An Atlas of North American Affairs

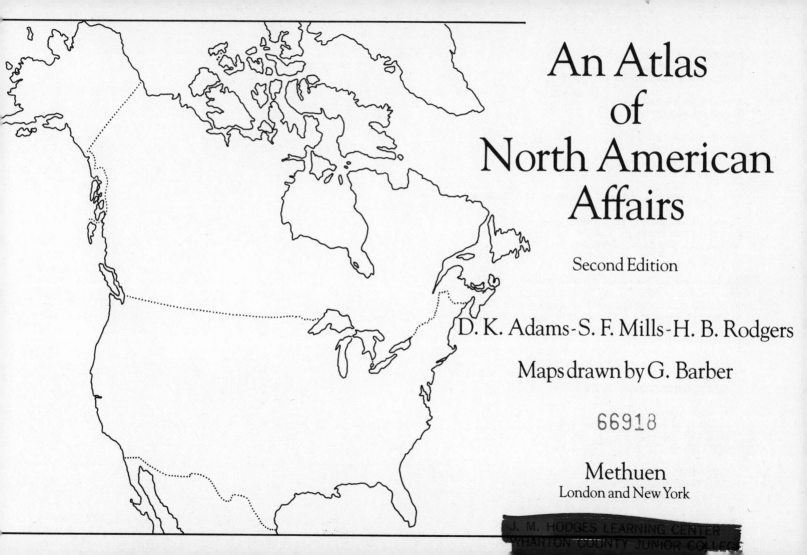

An Atlas
of
North American
Affairs

Second Edition

D. K. Adams · S. F. Mills · H. B. Rodgers

Maps drawn by G. Barber

66918

Methuen
London and New York

First published in 1969
by Methuen & Co. Ltd
11 New Fetter Lane, London EC4P 4EE

Reprinted three times
Second edition 1979

Published in the USA by
Methuen & Co. Ltd
in association with Methuen, Inc.
733 Third Avenue, New York, NY 10017

Typeset by Inforum Ltd, Portsmouth
Printed in Great Britain by
William Clowes & Sons Ltd, Beccles

British Library Cataloguing in Publication Data
Adams, David Keith
  An atlas of North American affairs.
  – 2nd ed.
  1. North America – Maps
  I. Title II. Mills, S F III. Rodgers, Harry
  Brian IV. Barber, Geoffrey, *b. 1927*
  912'.7   G1105   79–40760

  ISBN 0–416–85650–0
  ISBN 0–416–85640–3 Pbk

Contents

Foreword to first edition

No-one seeking to understand the forces that are shaping the contemporary world can ignore the two great nations of North America north of the Rio Grande. Sharing common interests, Canada and the United States have experienced parallel themes of national development: both were born of migration, and have grown to maturity through continuing mobility. The first section of this atlas presents a profile of the geographical environment within which development took place, and this is followed by consideration of crucial aspects of the westward movement. The original foundations of American prosperity lay in the fertility of the soil, and agriculture remains a great source of wealth. In the twentieth century, however, both nations have been transformed by large-scale industrialisation, and the atlas shows the distribution of raw materials, fuel and power resources, and manufacturing industry. Industrialisation produced urbanisation, and after a general review of city growth there are special studies of 'Megalopolis' and of Chicago. The transport systems serving the complex urban-industrial society are all treated in detail. Social problems in the United States are heightened by the presence of a large black minority, and particular attention is paid to Negro distribution, regional contrasts in wealth, and unequal educational opportunity. The atlas also explores the nature of political representation, and the strategic position of North America in a divided world.

We have worked primarily from basic statistical sources and official maps, and are indebted to the Departments of the United States Government, the St Lawrence Seaway Authority, and the Canadian High Commission in London for the provision of information. The translation of our ideas into finished maps owes much to the professional skills of our cartographer, Mr Geoffrey Barber. Our colleague Mr Anthony Brook was primarily responsible for Maps 46 and 47, and read the complete text with an acute eye and critical perception. Mr John Tyrrell assisted with some of the basic research. To our secretary, Miss Brenda Shufflebotham, who relieved many tensions with patience and unfailing sympathy, our gratitude is beyond measure.

Keele, 1968

D.K.A.
H.B.R.

Foreword to second edition

In preparing this second edition we have retained the existing format whilst updating the maps and texts where necessary. Some changes are therefore minor and unobtrusive; others are more radical, reflecting those aspects of North American life, such as the development of Alaskan oil, that have seen major changes during the past decade.

Keele, 1979

D.K.A.
S.F.M.

1 The physiographic regions of North America

The American continent north of the Rio Grande River embraces an area of about 7,000,000 square miles, politically divided at the 49th parallel, the Great Lakes and the St Lawrence between Canada and the United States. Despite its great size, however, North America has remarkable geological simplicity and can be divided into ten major structural regions.

In the north and east, covering more than half of Canada but extending only locally into the United States, is the old stable block of the Laurentian Shield (1). The hard, crystalline pre-cambrian rocks of the Shield have remained undisturbed over the greater part of the geological time scale. Eroded stumps of older mountains, for example the iron-rich Superior Highlands, cross its low and rolling surface; but only in the south and east, along the St Lawrence Valley and the Labrador coast, has recent uplift and tilting produced bold scarps and rugged mountains. Elsewhere the surface of the Shield is a low plateau, glacially scoured so that swells of bare rock drop to ice-eroded hollows filled with lakes or muskeg swamps. This multiplicity of lakes, large and small, is one of the most distinctive features of the Shield and a reminder that within this area were the two main centres of ice dispersion. Richly mineralised, the Shield is almost entirely without agricultural potential, although glacial clays fill some of the valley systems and the bleak shorelands south of Hudson Bay have a sedimentary cover.

South of the Shield palaeozoic sediments cover the pre-cambrian materials to form the Central Lowlands (2). These younger rocks lie almost undisturbed over great distances, with minor ripples locating the chief coal, oil and natural gas resources of the continent. Surface diversity here depends largely on the nature of the glacial cover. The youngest glacial clay-sheets form a smoothly rolling landscape traversed by rougher belts of moraine (2b). Further south both the older glacial 'drift' and the driftless areas (2c) have a more broken topography. Long salients of the Central Lowlands reach down the valleys of the Mackenzie (2a) and the St Lawrence.

To the west the palaeozoic and cretaceous sediments of the Central Lowlands are masked by a great sheet of younger, tertiary sediments deposited in a broad zone at the foot of the Rocky Mountains to form the Great Plains (3). Though flat and undissected, except by the west-east rivers, the Great Plains tilt up from the Mississippi to reach heights of over 5,000 feet at the base of the Rockies. In the north their smoothness is accentuated by glaciation (3a); in the central plains (3b), the edges of the tertiary overlay are fretted by erosion, sometimes producing 'badland' features.

The mountain ranges of North America form complex systems running parallel to the eastern and western coastlines. In the east the Appalachian system is flanked by the Atlantic Coast Plain (5a), a zone of scarps and vales modelled from dipping sedimentaries and descending to swampy coastal terraces. The Gulf Coast Plain (5b) is bisected by the alluvial slot of the lower Mississippi Valley (5c). From the Atlantic Coast Plain the land rises to form the Piedmont (4a), a rolling plateau at 1,000 feet to 1,500 feet built of pre-cambrian materials. At the junction of the Coast Plain and the Piedmont is the 'fall

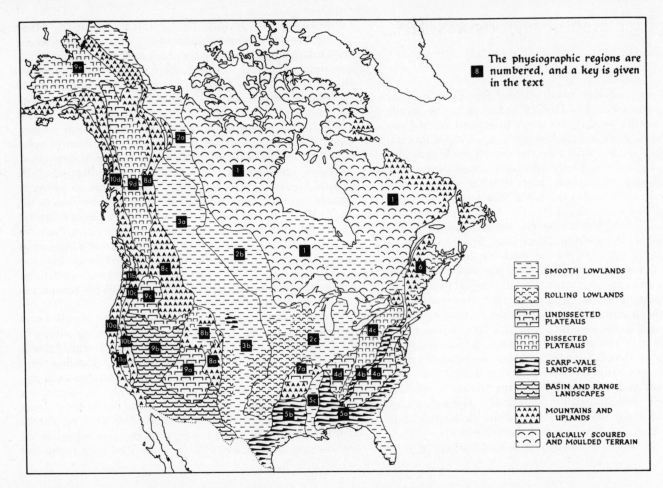

The physiographic regions are numbered, and a key is given in the text

Key:

- SMOOTH LOWLANDS
- ROLLING LOWLANDS
- UNDISSECTED PLATEAUS
- DISSECTED PLATEAUS
- SCARP-VALE LANDSCAPES
- BASIN AND RANGE LANDSCAPES
- MOUNTAINS AND UPLANDS
- GLACIALLY SCOURED AND MOULDED TERRAIN

1 » The physiographic regions of North America

line', where many of the rivers that drain the eastern seaboard tumble to the plain. This 'fall line' marked the head of navigation and provided sources of water power that partly explain the location of many early industrial sites. The inner western margin of the Piedmont is formed by the Blue Ridge, a bold forested ridge, linear in the north but to the south becoming the tangled upland mass of the Great Smokey Mountains. Beyond the Blue Ridge, in the Ridge and Valley province of the Appalachians (4b), folded palaeozoic sediments have been etched by erosion into a series of parallel crests rising above incised river valleys. These same sediments, further west, lie unfolded but uplifted as the Appalachian Plateau (4c) and, in a lower variant, the interior plateaux of southern Appalachia (4d). To the north the mountains of New England and Maritime Canada (6) are an extension of the Appalachians, distinguished especially by the glacial modelling of their landscape detail.

The mountain systems of western America are wider, higher and considerably more 'alpine' in appearance than those of the east, rising to over 14,000 feet. The basic structure of the Cordilleras consists of two parallel chains, the Rocky Mountains (8) and the Pacific ranges (10), separated by the Intermontane Plateaux (9). The Colorado Rockies (8a) are a simple double anticline, containing the high valleys known as the 'parks'. Although the Rockies (8a to 8d) are one of the world's longest and least broken mountain systems, extending from New Mexico to northern Alaska, they are almost severed by the Wyoming Basin (8b) through which the early routes to the west passed. The Intermontane Plateaux are characterised by great diversity of landscape: in the Colorado Plateau (9a) horizontal sedimentary strata are gashed by mile-deep canyons of which the Grand Canyon is merely the best known; the Columbia Plateau (9c) is partly covered by gently folded basaltic lava sheets. In the Basin and Range province (9b) desert basins of recent sedimentation are separated by upfaulted ridges carved by arid erosion into bizarre landforms. In the High Plateau of British Columbia (9d) glacial troughs and ribbon lakes dissect the surface, while in the far north the Intermontane Plateau province is occupied by the Yukon Basin of Alaska (9e). The Pacific mountains consist of two parallel ranges separated by a deep intervening valley. In California the Coast Range (10a) and the Sierra Nevada (10b) enclose the Central Valley of the Sacramento and the San Joaquin (11a). This pattern is continued to the north, with the Willamette valley-Puget Sound lowland (11b) separating the Cascade (10c) from the Coast Ranges. In Canada the central trough has been drowned, so that the Coast Ranges become the off-shore island chain and the Cascades the high and rugged coastal mountains of British Columbia and Alaska (10d).

2 Climatic contrast in North America

Despite immense climatic contrasts North America is also a continent of gentle climatic transitions. The bleak subarctic climates of the North contrast sharply with the warm, wet, winterless climate of Florida, yet nowhere is there an identifiable climatic 'break', only a gentle gradient of change. The absence of any significant east-west mountain barrier means that there is no American equivalent, in the climatic sense, of the Alps, and the transition from polar to tropical influences is subtle. Map 2 summarises the chief contrasts in the climatic distributions of North America by identifying a number of critically important climatic 'elements', key lines of rainfall and of temperature that together provide a broad guide to understanding regional differences.

Regional and seasonal contrasts in warmth are shown by two winter and two summer isotherms, or lines of equal temperature. The 50°F January isotherm, traversing the Gulf South, broadly demarcates that part of the South that has no real winter. In this mild coastal belt winter temperatures are well above the minimum for plant growth, frosts are rarely severe, and winter cropping is possible; the southern tip of Florida is frost free, and therefore virtually winterless. The 30°F January isotherm defines that part of the continent that has a hard winter in the sense that at least one month is persistently cold. So open is the interior of the continent to polar influences that this 30°F winter isotherm is pushed south as far as Missouri and Colorado; cities such as St Louis and Kansas City, in the same latitude as Lisbon and Athens, have prolonged spells of below-freezing temperatures in mid-winter. Looping to the south around the Rockies and the Sierra Nevada, the 30°F January isotherm then runs parallel to the Pacific coast, and is pushed so far to the north by the moderating influence of warm ocean currents that the coastlands of British Columbia are above freezing point in January. Unlike eastern ports on the St Lawrence, west-coast harbours such as Seattle and Vancouver are ice-free all the year round. North of this critical isotherm winters become progressively longer and harsher. The January temperature falls to a mean of −10°F in northern Saskatchewan, with daily minima of −40°F a commonplace, but much more important is the fact that winter lasts for eight months. Along the northern fringe of cultivation in the Prairie Provinces, the frost-free season is only 90 to 100 days, about the minimum for most kinds of extensive commercial agriculture. Further north is the zone of permafrost, continuous in the far North, broken but widespread over a considerable area of middle-northern Canada. Here the soil substratum is permanently frozen, so that surface soil becomes unworkable mud in the brief summer season.

Just as the polar airmass penetrates far to the south in the winter, the hot and humid Gulf airmass surges north during summer. The 60°F July isotherm runs in a north-westerly direction across settled Canada and then loops up towards the Arctic shore, with the result that the summer temperature of the Mackenzie lowlands, a frozen desert in winter, is no lower than that of Manchester, England. In relation to latitude the brief northern summer is relatively warm. The second July

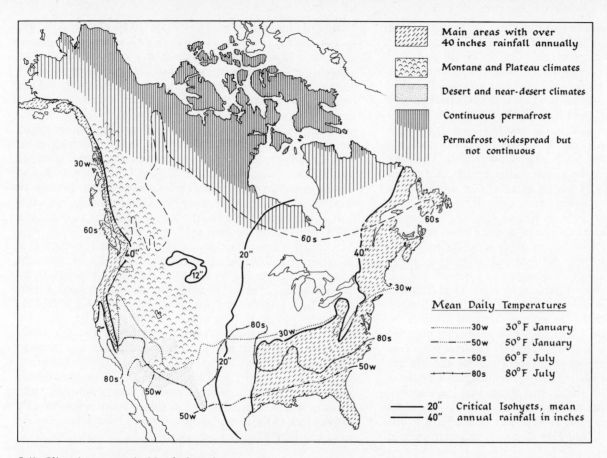

Legend:

Main areas with over 40 inches rainfall annually

Montane and Plateau climates

Desert and near-desert climates

Continuous permafrost

Permafrost widespread but not continuous

Mean Daily Temperatures

········30w   30° F January
·-·-·-·50w   50° F January
- - - -60s   60° F July
++++80s   80° F July

20"   Critical Isohyets, mean
40"   annual rainfall in inches

2 » Climatic contrast in North America

isotherm shown, that of 80°F, demonstrates that many parts of the south-east, south-west and south-central United States have very warm summers indeed. The 80°F July and 30°F January isotherms cross in the centre of the country: here is a perfect example of a climate of extremes associated with a continental interior; winters as cold as those of Central Europe are coupled with summers as warm as those of North Africa.

The other fundamental characteristic of climate is precipitation. The isohyet marking 40 inches of rain per annum roughly delimits the two areas of greatest rainfall. The long narrow ribbon along the west coast does not penetrate beyond the crest of the Sierra Nevada-Cascades, nor south of the Golden Gate. The larger eastern zone extends from Labrador into New England and then broadens to include the south-eastern and parts of the south-central states. However, by no means the whole of this area has an ample supply of moisture: west of the Mississippi the drought risk is serious, partly because of the high rate of evaporation in summer. Indeed, mean annual rainfall is only a crude guide to regional contrasts in humidity levels. This is clearly demonstrated by the climatic transition westward across the interior lowlands towards the Rocky Mountains. In the Mississippi valley rainfall is not only high (35 inches to 40 inches), but relatively constant from year to year so that serious droughts are rare. To the west conditions deteriorate: the annual variability of precipitation increases as the total decreases. This means that the annual 'expectation' may be as much as 25 per cent more or less than the long-term average, and in certain years rainfall will be marginal to the requirements for cultivation. This variability caused the ruin of many early farmers on the High Plains, who ploughed the sod in seasons of good rainfall only to find their land transformed into a dust bowl when the cycle of dry years returned.

In the far West mean annual rainfall is only about 15 inches on the Great Plains along the flanks of the mountains, and less than 12 inches in parts of Montana. Even in these conditions some low-yield grain cropping is possible, largely because most of the rain falls in the growing season, and winter snows are stored until spring. On the southern plains high mean annual totals are less effective since losses by evaporation are much higher, winter storage smaller, and the concentration of rainfall in the growing season is less pronounced. Because of these contrasts in the effectiveness of precipitation, no single isohyet can be used to show the 'drought barrier' to successful cultivation that is the threshold of the American West.

Western North America is a climatic mosaic. Contrasts in both rainfall and temperature reflect the dramatic relief pattern, so that landforms are the key to climate. The problem of the West is aridity. Sealed off from the moisture supply of both oceans by the north-south mountain ranges, the Great Basin of Utah and Nevada and the sheltered mountain valleys have less than 8 inches and approach desert conditions. Though rainfall increases northwards, and the Canadian Rockies are extremely wet, even the valleys in the High Plateau of British Columbia have a serious aridity problem. Much the most dramatic climatic transition in the whole continent occurs along the Sierra Nevada and the Cascades. In less than twenty miles from the eastern foot to the crest, rainfall increases from about 8 inches to as much as 80 inches per annum.

3 The major soil types of North America

This statement of the distribution of major soil types is necessarily very generalised, ignoring local contrasts and diversity. In the West, particularly, varied relief and dramatic climatic contrasts produce a fine mosaic of soils that defies summary on a small-scale map.

In general, climate and natural vegetation are the chief determinants of soil type; each major soil zone reflects a distinctive climatic and biotic environment. Over most of Canada soils are leached and show evidence of podsolisation, the dominant soil process where water percolation exceeds loss by run-off and evaporation. In such areas water seeps downwards, dissolving and removing the bases and humus, to leave the topsoil impoverished. True Podsols, varying locally, cover most of the Laurentian Shield and the New England uplands. Typically developed on loose glacial debris beneath coniferous forest, their upper horizons consist of acid grey sand, barren of humus and nutrients. Sterile and hungry soils, difficult to improve, these form some of the poorest agricultural land in North America. To the north, on the tundra fringe, the Podsols suffer the additional problem of permafrost.

South of the Podsols lie the Grey-Brown Podsolics, centred on the Ontario Peninsula of Canada, and extending south of Lake Erie and west beyond Lake Michigan. This zone is very variegated; beneath conifers, on coarse, freely drained, glacial sands, leaching is unimpeded and a near-podsol results; a few hundred yards away heavier clays may support Brown Forest soils, in which leaching is restricted by the less free-draining parent material. Buying land unseen was, and is, a gamble in this region.

In a zone reaching from southern New England to eastern Kentucky are the much better Brown Forest soils. Here, under deciduous forest cover yielding a richer humus supply, are soils with less pronounced leaching, partly because higher evaporation reduces the soil water surplus. The topsoil is darker, heavier, richer in nutrients and easier to improve.

In the south-eastern quadrant of North America are found the Red-Yellow Podsolics. In warmer conditions complex chemical changes produce a topsoil rich in iron and alumina, strongly coloured and often of clayey texture. Although many of the soil variants in this zone were originally highly fertile, few soils in America have been so abused by overproduction of demanding crops like cotton and tobacco. Exhaustion and erosion affect considerable areas in this zone.

The Prairie soils, roughly coterminous with the tall grass prairie, mark a transition from the soils of the humid east to those of the semi-arid West. Extremely fertile, they contain great reserves of grass humus in their dark upper horizons, although in places there is sufficient rainfall to produce signs of leaching. Unlike most grassland soils they suffer no serious drought risk; indeed water surplus is more often a problem than water deficit. On the level prairie interfluves, especially where clay-drift is the parent material, areas of Planosols occur. These are clay-pan soils in which leaching and drainage are impeded. Difficult to work, they are superbly productive soils when effectively drained. Planosols and Prairie soils form the

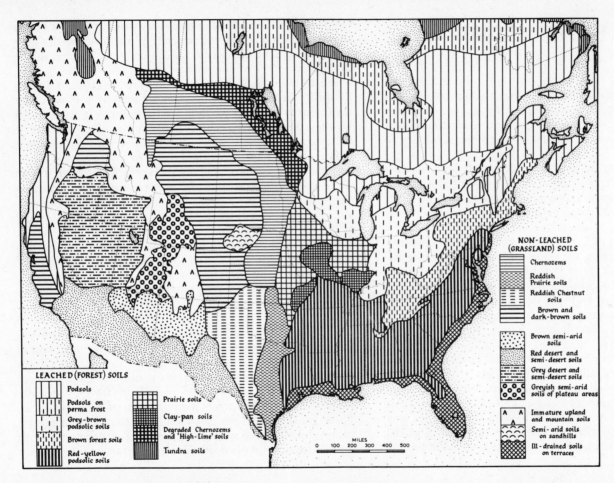

NON-LEACHED
(GRASSLAND) SOILS

Chernozems

Reddish
Prairie soils

Reddish Chestnut
soils

Brown and
dark-brown soils

Brown semi-arid
soils

Red desert and
semi-desert soils

Grey desert and
semi-desert soils

Greyish semi-arid
soils of plateau areas

Immature upland
and mountain soils

Semi-arid soils
on sandhills

Ill-drained soils
on terraces

LEACHED (FOREST) SOILS

Podsols

Podsols on
perma frost

Grey-brown
podsolic soils

Brown forest soils

Red-yellow
podsolic soils

Prairie soils

Clay-pan soils

Degraded Chernozems
and 'High-Lime' soils

Tundra soils

MILES

0   100 200 300 400 500

3 » The major soil types of North America

productive heart of the Corn Belt.

To the west of the Prairie soils is a zone of comparable fertility, that of the Black Earths, or Chernozems. Developed under tall grassland in a distinctly drier environment, and so less leached, these are blacker than the Prairie soils and contain immense original stores of humus in their surface layers, with an horizon of lime accumulation at depth. Phenomenally productive, they suffer greater drought hazards than the Prairie zone but are the pre-eminent wheat soils of the continent. To the north of the Chernozems, especially in Canada, is a transition from Black Earths to Podsols through a variety of intermediate types of degraded Chernozems, few of which are yet cultivated. South and west, in conditions of greater aridity, thinner grass cover and poorer reserves of humus, lie the Dark-Brown, or Chestnut, and the Reddish and Brown soils. The band of lime accumulation that is a feature of grassland soils becomes shallower, and on the threshold of the Mountain West comes to the surface as grey, semi-desert, highly alkaline soil.

The varied soils of the semi-arid West have many common characteristics. All are essentially mineral soils, lacking humus. Most are lightly coloured, with each particular colouration reflecting mineral composition: in southern areas high temperatures produce soil rich in alumina and iron oxides, giving a reddish colour.

The Brown and Dark-Brown soils of the natural grasslands re-occur in the Columbia Plateau and in central and southern California, but elsewhere in the West cultivation is restricted to irrigable valleys, and serious chemical problems are encountered in the use of these inorganic soils for irrigation agriculture. The soils of the wet Pacific coastlands are extremely variegated, and almost every soil type found on the continent is repeated in its appropriate climatic and biotic environment.

4 The natural vegetation of North America

Any map of the natural vegetation of a developed continent must be more an historical document than a description of present landscape. In North America, as elsewhere, the impact of man and his technology upon the environment has significantly changed the aspect of the land. Map 4 is relevant to contemporary America, particularly with respect to the forestry industry, a major activity and source of wealth, but the changes wrought by the myriad activities of man should not be forgotten. Throughout the period of white habitation forests have been cleared on an immense scale; huge areas of the central grasslands have gone under the plough; millions of cattle and sheep have grazed the high plains; semi deserts have been irrigated and made productive.

There were essentially four forms of natural vegetation in pre-European North America: the northern, eastern and western forests; the grasslands of the western half of the Mississippi basin, extending as dry variants into the western plateaux; the scrub, steppe and semi-desert vegetation of the arid West; and the treeless tundra of the far North.

The forests are most simply classified in terms of their location and tree species. The eastern forests consisted largely of Oak woodland, containing a variety of subordinate species such as Chestnut, Poplar, Maple and Hickory. Some conifers were to be found on poorer soils, on high ground, and in the northern part of this zone. Conifers also dominated the South-East: after an Oak-Pine transitional belt they largely replaced Oak on the limited soils of the coast plain to form the

southern Pine forests, where a warm climate enables sufficiently rapid growth for timber to be treated as a crop. The boreal or northern forest of Canada, an immense tract of woodland of which only the accessible south-eastern fringe has been widely worked, shows considerable botanical contrast. Hardwoods and magnificent stands of Red and White Pine, now largely felled, were the principal commercial attraction in the South-East. But to the north the boreal forest becomes poorer, dominated by Spruce, Balsam, Fir and Birch, with progressively more stunted growth finally giving way to the treeless tundra. To the west also the Canadian forests become relatively poor and less attractive, as well as less accessible for commercial exploitation. Along the Pacific coast forest cover faithfully reflects contrasts in rainfall. On the wet coastal slopes of the Pacific ranges fine stands of Douglas Fir, a superb economic resource, give way northwards to Sitka Spruce and are flanked to the south by the Redwood forests of California. On the drier and often higher and inaccessible slopes of the Cascades, Sierra Nevada and Rocky Mountains are Ponderosa and Lodgepole Pine of commercial value.

The grasslands of the interior lowlands originally took two forms, the tall grass prairie and the short grass steppe. The former, extending into areas so humid that it is something of a botanical enigma why they should carry grassland and not forest, formed a broad wedge tapering into Illinois and covering most of the present grain states and provinces. On the Great Plains, the change in climate is reflected in the transition from tall to short grass. The greater aridity of the intermontane plateaux results in degeneration to semi-desert scrub, dominated by sage, creosote and saltbush. True deserts are of very limited extent: the largest is in north-west Utah, while the south-western deserts are, botanically, not deserts at all.

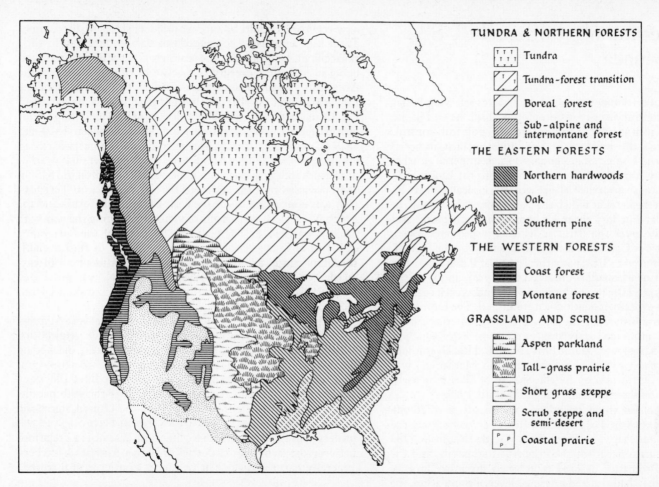

TUNDRA & NORTHERN FORESTS

- Tundra
- Tundra-forest transition
- Boreal forest
- Sub-alpine and intermontane forest

THE EASTERN FORESTS

- Northern hardwoods
- Oak
- Southern pine

THE WESTERN FORESTS

- Coast forest
- Montane forest

GRASSLAND AND SCRUB

- Aspen parkland
- Tall-grass prairie
- Short grass steppe
- Scrub steppe and semi-desert
- Coastal prairie

4 » The natural vegetation of North America

5 The territorial growth of the USA and Canada

The history of settlement in the United States (cf. Map 8) has been one of continuous expansion within, until the end of the nineteenth century, an expanding area of political control. Although itself the product of revolution against imperial domination, the United States engaged in an imperial process that eventually brought many new states into the Union. On Map 5 the stages of territorial growth are indicated, I to X, together with the dates at which the states joined the Union. In Canada similar but less complex expansion took place, and Map 5 merely gives the dates at which the provinces were organised. Lower Canada was originally settled by the French, but was transferred to Britain by the Treaty of Paris, 1763. The borders of British Canada were fixed by negotiation with the United States after the Revolutionary War, and as each country expanded the process of negotiation continued. The Dominion of Canada, established by the British North America Act of 1867, at first embraced only the four provinces of Quebec, Ontario, New Brunswick and Nova Scotia. This Dominion, enlarged by the western provinces and the Maritimes, was given legislative autonomy by the Statute of Westminster in 1931. Newfoundland remained separate until 1949.

When the claim to independence was made in 1776 the United States consisted of the tier of British colonies along the Atlantic seaboard (I). The Peace Treaty with Britain in 1783 extended the national frontier to the Mississippi (II); and the Northwest Ordinance of 1787 established the procedure by which, after they had reached a defined level of population, the new territories could be incorporated as states of the Union. Thereafter, expansion continued through a mixture of historical accident, land hunger, the search for 'natural' frontiers, and belief in 'manifest destiny' – a sense of mission to carry the American system beyond the frontier. The vast area of the Louisiana Purchase (III) was bought from France by agents of President Jefferson in 1803. Florida (IV), including West Florida (A, B), was acquired from Spain between 1810 and 1819. Texas (V), formerly a part of the Spanish–Mexican empire, rebelled against Mexico in 1836, and after nine years of precarious independence was annexed to the Union in 1845. In 1846 possession of the southern part of the Oregon Territory (VI) was confirmed by treaty with Britain. California and the South-West (VII) were fruits of victory following the war with Mexico of 1846-8. The Gadsden Purchase of the Gila valley (VIII) in 1853 was motivated by the desire to find a viable southern route for the projected transcontinental railway. Alaska (IX), 'the ice-box of North America', was purchased from Russia in 1867. Sovereignty over the Hawaiian Islands (X) was assumed in 1898.

During this period of national expansion there were frequent border disputes between the United States and its neighbours, and the boundaries of the territorial acquisitions are marked on the map in their final negotiated form. The Adams-Onis Transcontinental Treaty of 1819, for example, fixed the western border of the Louisiana Purchase; in 1818 the 49th parallel was established as the frontier between the United States and Canada from the Great Lakes to the Oregon Territory, and was projected to the Pacific in 1846. Since the War of 1812 relations between the two great countries of North America have been generally harmonious; their common frontier is unfortified.

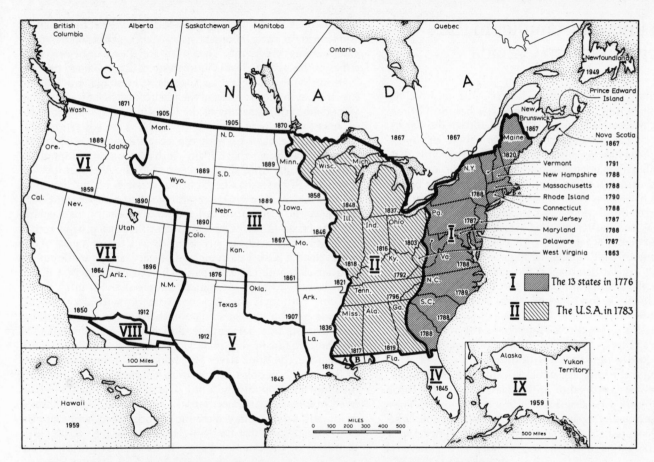

Legend within map:

British Columbia
Alberta
Saskatchewan
Manitoba
Quebec

Ontario

C A N A D A

Newfoundland
1949

Prince Edward Island

New Brunswick 1867

Nova Scotia 1867

1871 Wash.
1905 Mont.
1905
1870
N.D.
1867
1867

Maine 1820

1889 Ore.
1889 Idaho
Wyo.
1889 Minn.
1889 S.D.
Wisc.
Mich.

Cal.
1859
Nev.
1890
Utah
1890 Colo.
Nebr.
1889 Iowa
1858
Ill.
1848
Ind.
1837
Ohio
1803

N.Y. 1788

Pa. 1787

1788

Vermont 1791
New Hampshire 1788
Massachusetts 1788
Rhode Island 1790
Connecticut 1788
New Jersey 1787
Maryland 1788
Delaware 1787
West Virginia 1863

I

VII

VI

III

1864 Ariz.
1896
N.M.
1876
Kan.
1867 Mo.
1861
1846
1816
Ky.
1792
1818
II
1821
Tenn.
1796

Va. 1788

N.C. 1789

1850
1912
Okla.
Ark.
1836
Miss.
Ala.
Ga.
1788

S.C. 1788

VIII

Texas
1912
V
La.
1907
1817
1819
1812
A B
Fla.

IV
1845

I — The 13 states in 1776
II — The U.S.A. in 1783

Inset left:
100 Miles
Hawaii
1959

Inset right:
Alaska
Yukon Territory
IX
1959

MILES
0 100 200 300 400 500

500 Miles

5 » Territorial growth of the USA and Canada. *The major stages in the territorial growth of the USA are shown, I to X, together with the dates of accession of states to the Union. In Canada the dates are those at which provinces were admitted to the Dominion*

6 Indian linguistic families in the USA and southern Canada

When Columbus sailed westward from Cadiz in 1492 he believed that he would find a sea route to the East, to Cathay and the Indies. Making landfall among the islands of the Caribbean he believed that he had reached his destination, and in his delusion called the natives 'Indians'. However, the name that he gave the indigenous peoples of the American continent was not entirely incorrect, for they were descendants of the bands of Mongoloid tribesmen who, between 10,000 and 25,000 BC had crossed over the Bering Strait from Asia.

At their peak in the fifteenth and sixteenth centuries these 'Indians' numbered perhaps between 600,000 and 800,000, although estimates have ranged as high as twelve to fifteen million. Their diverse languages and cultures have always made classification difficult, but rigorous anthropological analysis by scholars such as Powell, Wissler and Kroeber has resulted in a general classification in terms of linguistic stock. Map 6 indicates the broad distribution of the seven major groups, and also those areas in which the dominant tribes fell outside these loose linguistic classifications.

The Algonquian group (1), which includes the Algonquin, Ottawa, Shawnee, Arapaho and Blackfoot, were those encountered by the first English and French explorers. They were a semi-nomadic, agricultural and hunting people who lived in bark-covered, dome-shaped wigwams, had developed the birch-bark canoe and the snow-shoe, and cultivated squash, maize and tobacco. These Indians were at first friendly and taught the early colonists many of their skills. Such famous chieftains as Massasoit, Tecumseh and Pontiac belonged to tribes of this group. The Iroquoian stock (2) contained the Five Nations (Mohawk, Cayuga, Oneida, Onondaga and Seneca), together with the Huron and the Cherokee. The Siouan group (3) included the Catawba of the Carolinas, and Plains Indians such as the Crow and the Dakota who were truly nomadic, living off the buffalo, with the portable tepee as their traditional dwelling. These Plains Indians quickly adopted the horse after its introduction into North America by the Spaniards. The Caddoans (5) of the western plains, including the Pawnee, in many ways resembled their Sioux neighbours. The Muskhogean nations of the South-East (4), particularly the Choctaw, Creek, Chickasaw and Seminole, were settled agriculturalists with an economy based upon maize. They were adept at basket weaving and pottery, and were organised into an elaborate caste system. The Apache and Navaho of Athapascan stock (6) dominated much of the south-western plateau. Although the Apache were nomadic hunters, the Navaho economy was based upon sheep herding and farming, and they became particularly skilled weavers of wool. The Shoshonean group (7) included such varied nations as the Comanche, the Wind River Shoshone of Wyoming, and many of the Pueblo peoples of the south-western desert, including the Hopi and possible the Zuni. The sedentary Pueblo Indians lived in dense 'apartment houses', or Pueblos, built of stone, wood and adobe. They were highly organised, and were the only Indians north of the Rio Grande to weave cotton cloth. Rumours of the Pueblos gave rise to the myth of the Seven

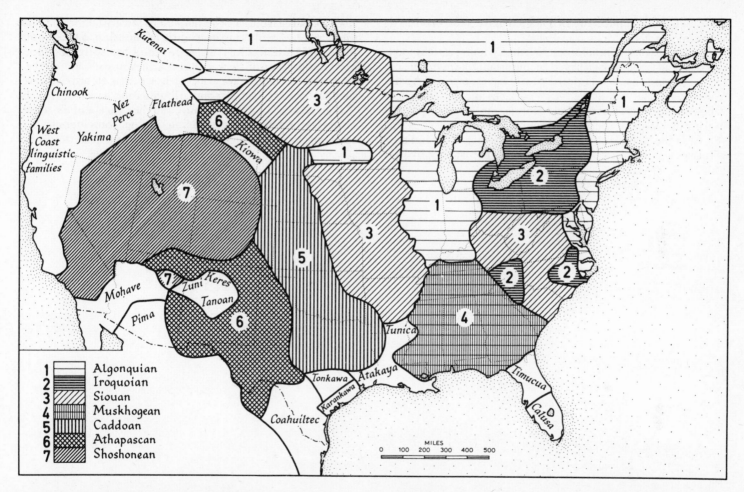

Kurenai

Chinook

Nez
Perce

Flathead

West
Coast
linguistic
families

Yakima

Kiowa

6

7

Mohave

7

Zuni Keres

Pima

Tanoan

6

1

1

3

1

5

3

Tunica

1

2

3

2

2

Timucua

Calusa

Tonkawa

Atakaya

Karankawa

Coahuiltec

4

MILES
0 100 200 300 400 500

1		Algonquian
2		Iroquoian
3		Siouan
4		Muskhogean
5		Caddoan
6		Athapascan
7		Shoshonean

6 » Indian linguistic families in the USA and southern Canada

Cities of Cibola, supposedly rich in golden treasure, that lured Coronado to New Mexico in 1540.

The culture of the Indians was rich in mythology. Religious practices and ceremonials played an important role in the life of the tribes, and many traditional rituals have survived. Apart from small reservations in New York, in the St Lawrence valley and in South Carolina and Florida, most contemporary Indians live west of the Mississippi on reservations (cf. Map 48). After the coming of the white man the story of the Indians was largely one of war and expropriation. Thrust back by the advance of the frontier of settlement to the least desirable land, their present distribution bears little relationship to the original locational pattern. Only in recent years has there developed new recognition of their cultural achievements and of their contribution to the history of North America. Research centres such as those at Santa Fé and Albuquerque have stressed the 'Americanness' of Indian culture, and the concept of the 'noble savage' is finding new meaning in the contemporary re-assessment of the role of minority groups in America.

7 Geographical obstacles to the expansion of settlement in the USA

Each phase of the advance of the frontier of settlement between 1650 and 1890 was shaped and guided by geographical features. In the southern colonies the first obstacle was the fall line, where the soft sedimentaries of the Coast Plain give way to the hard crystalline rocks of the Piedmont. A line of falls and rapids, it marked the head of navigation of the Atlantic rivers and for a time limited the export-orientated economy of Virginia to the tidewater. When settlement spread on to the Piedmont the fall line became a social divide separating the large plantations of the tidewater from the pioneer farms of the 'Old West'. Further north the fall line is submerged, and in New England and upstate New York the chief barriers were the glaciated uplands of the Green, White and Adirondack Mountains (1, 2). The fertile valleys that lay within them soon reached and passed their population peak, and by the 1820s showed signs of progressive rural depopulation.

The Piedmont (cf. Map 1) terminates to the west in the bold wooded line of the Blue Ridge, which presented an almost impassable obstacle to early settlers. Between 1690 and 1760, colonists entering the Appalachians from the Virginian and Pennsylvanian tidewater passed either round or through gaps in the northern Blue Ridge, to find themselves imprisoned between it and the parallel system of interior Appalachia. The new northern routes across the scarp of the Appalachian Plateau (3, 4), and the Greenbrier gap further south (5), led before 1763 into French territory. English colonists were therefore deflected to the Cumberland Gap (6), a natural route west that had been used for centuries by Indians and was pioneered by Daniel Boone's parties in the 1760s and 1770s.

The Midwest is endowed with a generous network of navigable rivers. These not only carried settlers to the far frontier, but also transported their produce to eastern and European markets. The major route passed down the Ohio-Mississippi system, by raft and river boat, to the trans-shipment port of New Orleans. Although the Mississippi could be navigated almost to the Superior Highlands (7), the upper reaches of most midwestern rivers quickly became too shallow for navigation. The vast region without water transport was at first dominated by the covered wagon, but it was not fully exploited until the coming of the railroad.

The drought barrier to western farming and compact settlement is often taken to be the 100th meridian, but this is an arbitrary location for a broad transitional zone from humid to semi-arid conditions. The eastern edge of the Great Plains is marked by a ragged escarpment, behind which the plains roll westward to the Rocky Mountains. Streams are intermittent, and frequently end in salt flats. Since moisture losses by evaporation increase southwards, no single isohyet can be taken to mark the drought barrier, and therefore parts of three isohyets are shown on Map 7. These mark the western limits of the main area of cropland.

The front ranges of the Rocky Mountains rise to more than 12,000 feet, but were less formidable than expected. Between

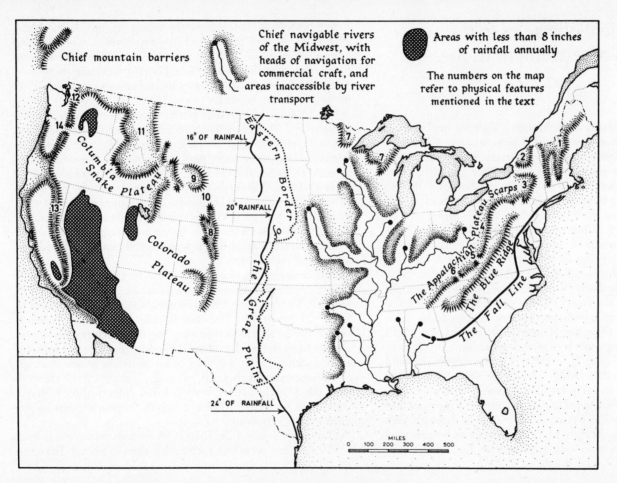

Chief mountain barriers

Chief navigable rivers of the Midwest, with heads of navigation for commercial craft, and areas inaccessible by river transport

Areas with less than 8 inches of rainfall annually

The numbers on the map refer to physical features mentioned in the text

16" OF RAINFALL

20" RAINFALL

24" OF RAINFALL

Eastern Border of the Great Plains

Columbia Snake Plateau

Colorado Plateau

The Appalachian Plateau Scarps

The Blue Ridge

The Fall Line

MILES
0 100 200 300 400 500

7 » Geographical obstacles to the expansion of settlement in the USA

the Colorado Rockies (8) and the Big Horn and Wind River Ranges (9) lies the Wyoming Basin and South Pass (10). Through this broad and easy corridor to the West passed the pioneer trails (cf. Map 9) followed by most of the settlers travelling by land to the West Coast between 1830 and 1870. The broader, more complex patterns of the Northern Rockies (11) were not seriously violated until the coming of the transcontinental railroad (cf. Map 10). Beyond South Pass the Snake led directly to the Columbia gap (14) through the Cascades (12). Further south the barriers that lay behind the Rockies presented a more serious challenge than the mountains themselves. Most of the streams of the Colorado Plateau are deeply incised; above these canyons the plateau is semi-desert. In the Great Basin of Utah and Nevada salt lakes and flats abound in an otherwise almost waterless area, making passage extremely hazardous. The last great obstacle on the way to California was one of the most difficult to cross. The eastern wall of the Great Valley is formed by the unbroken ridge of the Sierra Nevada (13), and the southern route around the mountains meant crossing the south-western deserts. One of the few direct routes through the Sierras lies through the Donner Pass: high enough to be snowbound in winter, it was named after the disastrous Donner party of 1846, some of whom survived only by eating the flesh of those of their comrades who died.

8 The advance of the frontier of settlement in the USA

The earliest permanent settlements by English colonists within the present boundaries of the United States were made at widely separated sites along the Atlantic coast. Jamestown was founded in 1607 on a marshy, malarial peninsula jutting into the estuary of the James River. From this nucleus in Virginia, a narrow ribbon of thinly dispersed settlement followed the intricate system of navigable rivers opening into Chesapeake Bay. It was, however, only a coastal façade masking an interior populated by scattered Indian tribes. White colonisation clung to the coastline; the commercial farms, from which the 'plantations' were to evolve, practised cash-crop cultivation of tobacco which was loaded at natural anchorages, or landings, for direct shipment to England.

Much further north, on the indented coastline of Massachusetts Bay, other settlements were made at Plymouth (1620), Salem (1628) and Boston (1630). Founded by nonconformist exiles from England, these group colonies of Pilgrims and Puritans were nucleated port-villages that quickly multiplied by internal division as well as through reinforcement by new arrivals. The process of penetration into the interior began with movement into the Connecticut and Merrimack valleys.

Between these two distinct areas of English colonisation lay a middle zone in which the earliest settlements were made by Dutch and Swedes. New Amsterdam, a tiny walled town on the tip of Manhattan Island, was the finest base along the entire Atlantic coast. At the head of the Delaware estuary lay the less successful Swedish colony of Fort Christina, soon to be acquired by the Dutch.

From these, and other primary colonies in the Carolinas, settlement expanded so that by 1700 scattered European settlements stretched from southern Maine to South Carolina, clinging to navigable water. In this 'tidewater phase' the European invaders had secured little more than a beachhead on the continent. Tentative penetration had begun in New England; colonists were beginning to stream into the hinterland of Philadelphia; and in Viginia settlers were already moving on to the Piedmont.

Quicker progress into the 'wilderness' was made between 1700 and 1750. Most of the fertile valleys of south-eastern New England were occupied, and a finger of settlement reached west along the Mohawk valley of upstate New York. This was a precocious advance, halted by Indian resistance, and by the political barrier of the Anglo-French frontier. Deeper penetration was made in Pennsylvania, where a liberal immigration policy encouraged many more settlers of varied ethnic stock. The rolling hill country of south-eastern Pennsylvania became thickly settled, and the frontier reached the Appalachians, the first major obstacle to settlement (cf. Map 7). The main line of advance was guided by the physical grain of the Appalachian ridges to the south-west, along the twin forks of the Shenandoah into the Virginia back-country. Further south, interior advance was slower, and was confined chiefly to the terraces of the major rivers, such as the Santee and the Savannah.

Between 1750 and 1790, by contrast, the frontier moved

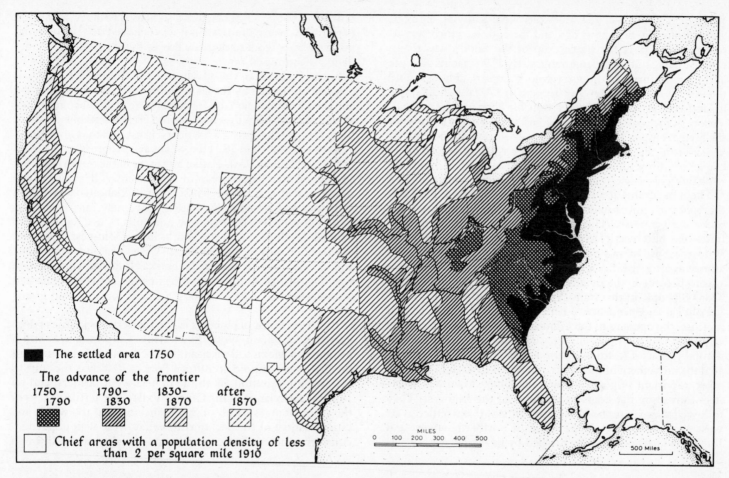

■ The settled area 1750

The advance of the frontier

| 1750–1790 | 1790–1830 | 1830–1870 | after 1870 |

Chief areas with a population density of less
than 2 per square mile 1910

MILES
0 100 200 300 400 500

500 Miles

8 » The advance of the frontier of settlement in the USA

faster in the South. Tidewater soils were showing signs of exhaustion, but European demand for cotton, which was to replace tobacco as the staple crop of the South, was rising rapidly. The South was land hungry. By 1790 eastern Georgia and the Carolina back-country were occupied, although until the invention of Whitney's cotton gin in 1793 the short staple upland cotton was much less valuable than the 'sea island' variety of the coastal plantations. Further north the collapse of the French empire brought a 'land rush' into western Pennsylvania. From the new frontier of Pittsburgh a flood of settlers began to move down the Ohio, and what had been the Mohawk cul-de-sac was now opened to Lake Ontario.

The most dramatic advance of the frontier before 1790 was the bold movement under men like Daniel Boone into Kentucky and Tennessee. This country of fertile basins set amongst limestone hills was reached by the long journey along the Wilderness Road and through the Cumberland Gap. It was almost as attractive to eighteenth-century pioneers as Oregon was to become in the nineteenth century. By 1800 there were 326,000 people in this trans-Appalachian outlier.

Political independence, greater immigration and natural increase, the opening of the Ohio and Mississippi systems, the acquisition of the Louisiana Purchase, the absence of serious natural obstacles to midwestern settlement: these all accelerated the movement of the frontier between 1790 and 1830. The most important single factor was the Ohio, down which settlers moved on flat-boats to the heart of the Midwest. They followed the river to the Mississippi-Missouri and settled as far west as Kansas City. Large areas of northern Indiana and Illinois, which could not be reached by navigable waterways,

remained empty. Other factors also helped to delay settlement of the midwestern prairies, for it was believed that land that did not bear trees would not grow crops; this barrier of prejudice deflected immigration.

In the South, too, the advance of the frontier by 1830 was directly influenced by the accessibility of water transportation and the growth of demand for cotton. From coastal nuclei such as Mobile, and from the cluster of old French settlements about New Orleans, long riverine salients thrust into the Gulf Plains.

Between 1830 and 1870 the westward progress of the frontier was relatively slow. Earlier advances in the South had been so ragged that large areas of land were still available for development east of the Mississippi; Oklahoma was Indian Territory and closed to the settler; movement into Texas was largely confined to the eastern woodlands. The Civil War also slowed development in the South. In the Midwest, however, the frontier moved into southern Wisconsin and Minnesota, and across Iowa to eastern Nebraska. Railroad construction was the great stimulus, for the companies actively sponsored immigration in order to dispose of their massive land grants (cf. Map 10).

By 1870 groups of pioneers had made perilous journeys deep into the Mountain West. Even while California was still a province of Mexico, Americans had begun to acquire land; but the discovery of gold at Sutter's Fort in 1848 was the spur to massive immigration. With the miners went farmers, and by 1870 the farm lands of the Central Valley, the fertile valleys of the Coast Ranges south of San Francisco, and the wheat and cattle country of the Sacramento valley were well populated. Another coherent line of settlement stretched north through the Willamette and Columbia valleys at the end of the Oregon Trail (cf. Map 9). In Utah the Mormon colony had been firmly planted at the foot of the Wasatch Mountains, and a chain of settlements extended south to form the 'Mormon corridor'.

After 1870 farmers spread into the Great Plains, from the Dakotas to Texas. Much of this semi-arid grassland, the 'Great American Desert' of the mid-nineteenth century, had been used for ranching since the 1860s, but only with the ramification of the railroads was arable farming established. Large areas of the Mountain West remained relatively unpopulated, except where mining had become extensive.

9 The growth of communications in the USA: rivers, canals and western trails

The westward movement of the frontier of settlement was accompanied by the development of a communications system linking it with the main areas of population to the East. The early Appalachian frontier was joined to the Atlantic seaboard by primitive roads that had in part a military function, and stategic needs were to contribute to the progressive development of communications throughout the national period. Across the Appalachians, navigable rivers facilitated exploitation of the central lowlands, and commercial traffic was at first focussed on New Orleans, the natural outlet of the entire central basin. Canal construction later linked the upper Ohio with the Great Lakes; from them the Erie Canal gave passage to the Hudson valley, and the arteries of trade and commerce swung from a north-south to a west-east axis, a factor tending to strengthen the political allegiance of the new western territories to the Union. Beyond the Mississippi the absence of navigable rivers dictated reliance on land transport. Frontier communications thus passed through a variety of phases, each dominated by a particular form of transport. The coming of the railroads again changed the pattern (cf. Maps 10, 31), and the process has continued with the proliferation of air-routes and superhighways (cf. Maps 33, 34).

The great waterway of the Mississippi was navigable in the early nineteenth century from the Gulf to falls below the present cities of Minneapolis and St Paul. From some of its upper tributaries portages led to Lakes Superior and Michigan. The Ohio and the Missouri differed in their commercial possibilities. Although the falls of the Ohio at Louisville were an obstacle, the river was navigable beyond Pittsburgh, and major tributaries, such as the Tennessee, offered routes into southern Appalachia. The Missouri was much less valuable. Beyond Leavenworth only seasonal navigation was possible; in spring and early summer small steamboats could reach upstream as far as Fort Benton, but regular commercial service was impossible.

The South was generally well endowed with navigable rivers. The Arkansas and Red Rivers helped to open up the new cotton lands west of the Mississippi. Mobile lay at the mouth of the Alabama River and prospered on the cotton of its hinterland. The Chattahoochee, the Savannah and other rivers along the Gulf Coast and the south-eastern seaboard assisted the spread of cotton in the Lower South. The South relied so much upon water transport, which was adequate for its needs, that railroads only developed slowly (cf. Map 10).

In 1825 the Erie Canal was opened from Albany to Buffalo on Lake Erie. This development confirmed New York's commercial supremacy by opening up the midwestern hinterland to the city's trade. However, the canal did not reach the densely settled and productive valley of the Ohio, and by the 1830s a number of schemes (see inset) had been launched to link the valley with the Great Lakes and hence indirectly with New York. The Wabash and Erie Canal crossed northern Indiana to Toledo, which was also connected by the Miami and Erie

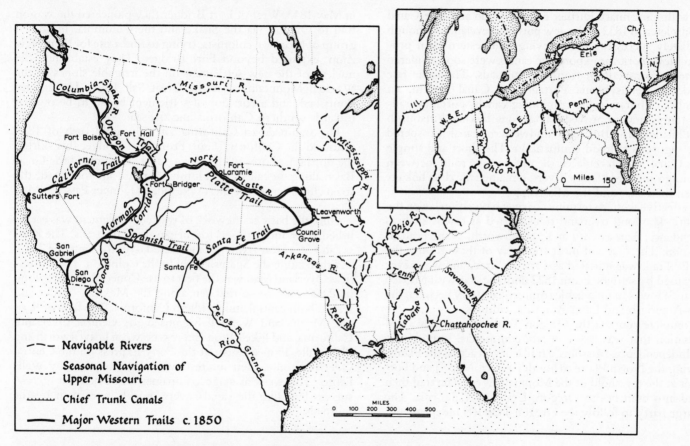

Map labels

Columbia-Snake R.
Missouri R.
Fort Boise
Fort Hall
Oregon Trail
California Trail
Sutters Fort
Fort Bridger
North Platte R.
Fort Laramie
Platte Trail
Mormon Corridor
Spanish Trail
Santa Fe Trail
Leavenworth
Council Grove
Mississippi R.
Ohio R.
San Gabriel
San Diego
Colorado R.
Santa Fe
Arkansas R.
Tenn. R.
Savannah R.
Pecos R.
Red R.
Alabama R.
Chattahoochee R.
Rio Grande

Inset labels
Ch.
W. Erie
N.
Ill.
W. & E.
M. & E.
O. & E.
Penn.
Ohio R.
0 Miles 150

Legend
–·– Navigable Rivers
····· Seasonal Navigation of Upper Missouri
········· Chief Trunk Canals
▬▬ Major Western Trails c.1850

MILES
0 100 200 300 400 500

9 » The growth of communications in the USA: rivers, canals and western trails. *In the inset the following canals are indicated by initial letter: the Wabash and Erie (W & E), Miami and Erie (M & E), Ohio and Erie (O & E), Northampton (N), Champlain (Ch)*

Canal with Cincinnati. Further east the Ohio and Erie Canal was completed in 1832 to the new port of Cleveland. Although immediately successful in conveying midwestern farm produce to New York for export, the canals were soon rendered obsolete by competition from the railroads. The same fate awaited the Pennsylvania Portage and Canal system, an impossibly elaborate route combining canals, portages, railroads, ramps and improved navigations linking Pittsburgh with Philadelphia. But one midwestern canal prospered despite vigorous railroad competition. The short and simple Illinois Canal, which replaced the old portage route between the Chicago and Des Plaines Rivers, remained the chief linkage between the Lakes and the Mississippi.

The effective western terminus of river navigation lay on the Missouri. The long overland trails started at towns such as Independence, Kansas City and Leavenworth, at the head of navigation. The first and most southerly of these routes, the Sante Fe Trail, was initiated as a traders' trail, and was never greatly used by settlers. From 1822 until the war with Mexico (cf. Map 5) it was an invaluable commercial artery between the Anglo-American and Latin-American cultures.

In complete contrast the Oregon Trail was a routeway of colonisation that was never of any commercial importance. From Independence, Missouri, a trail led west across the Plains, following the North Platte to South Pass (cf. Map 7) and Fort Bridger at the threshold of the Mountain West. The trail then divided into branches to Oregon, Utah and California. The first large party to follow the Oregon Trail left Independence in May 1843. West of Fort Bridger they pioneered the wagon trail to Oregon via the Snake and the Columbia. In 1847 a group of Mormon colonists, trying to find a site for their New Zion, explored beyond Fort Bridger. They established the nucleus of the new settlement on the irrigable slopes of the Wasatch Mountains near the Great Salt Lake. The colony flourished, and a corridor of settlement began to be pushed towards southern California and the sea.

The stampede to California after the gold rush of 1849 followed the California Trail. From Fort Bridger this skirted the northern shores of the Great Salt Lake, crossed the Great Basin along the line of the Humboldt river, and then made the steep climb across the Sierra Nevada at Donner Pass (cf. Map 7).

Once the basic framework of western settlement was established, overland mail services began along the trails. The Kansas and Stockton Express Line passed over the Santa Fe Trail, and then along the Spanish Trail to the Colorado. The Butterfield Overland Mail was the first to use Concord coaches along its 2,800-mile route that ran along the Mexican border and served both central and southern California. The firm of Russell, Majors and Waddell organised the Central Overland, California, and Pike's Peak Express between Leavenworth and Placerville. Pioneers also of the Pony Express on the Central Overland route, their interests were later acquired by Wells Fargo. The western stage companies had brief commercial success but, like the canals, were quickly overtaken by the railroads.

10 The growth of communications in the USA: railroads 1860, and the transcontinental lines 1900

The first scheduled steam-hauled rail service opened in South Carolina in 1830, and by 1860 a network of lines had spread over the United States east of the Mississippi. They followed the population dispersion patterns (cf. Map 8), and track mileage increased rapidly from 9,000 miles in 1850 to 30,626 in 1860. By 1860 the rails had followed settlement into Iowa and Missouri, but generally throughout the trans-Mississippi west they preceded close settlement, opened up the Great Plains (cf. Maps 7, 9) and, after 1869, effectively linked the eastern states with the west coast.

The eastern railroad pattern reflected not merely the distribution of population but also the socio-economic structure of the nation. Development was at first slow in areas near navigable water, but even here the advantages of the new method of transportation quickly ensured its success. Where water navigation was inadequate, the railroads quickly became dominant (cf. Map 9). The South, with relatively sparse population and shortage of capital, lagged behind; its major crop, cotton, provided only seasonal freight and could easily be carried by water. Despite this railroads were reaching from Charleston towards New Orleans by 1860 and, although designed to tap midwestern trade rather than carry local southern products, a rail link had been forged between New Orleans and Chicago. Throughout the country most lines were short, but interconnections common. By 1850 continuous travel was possible between Maine and the Great Lakes, a four-day journey; by 1860 through-travel was possible as far west as Kansas City in little more than a week, whereas before the coming of the railroad a similar expedition would have taken well over a month.

The steady westward pressure of farmers in search of cheap land, the discovery of gold in California, belief that the Orient offered a trading area ripe for exploitation, and strategic factors inherent in the expansion of the Union combined to produce demand for construction of a transcontinental railroad. In 1850 congress had passed a land grant act to stimulate construction of the line from the Lakes to the Gulf by offering land from the public domain free to the states along the proposed right-of-way. Both the federal and state governments followed this precedent for the next half century, and land grants were of particular importance in relation to the transcontinentals.

In 1862 President Lincoln authorised the construction of a Pacific railroad from Omaha to Sacramento. The Union Pacific was to build west from the Missouri and the Central Pacific east from California. Each company was given a financial subsidy and massive land grants along the proposed route. Despite Indian attack, difficult terrain, shortage of supplies and financial mismanagement the railroad was built. The two lines met at Promontory Point, Utah, on 10 May 1869. Other transcontinentals followed, stimulated perhaps not so much by anticipated operating profits as by the rich spoils of construction. A Northern Pacific Railroad was planned as early as 1864, and received federal grants to build west from Lake Superior.

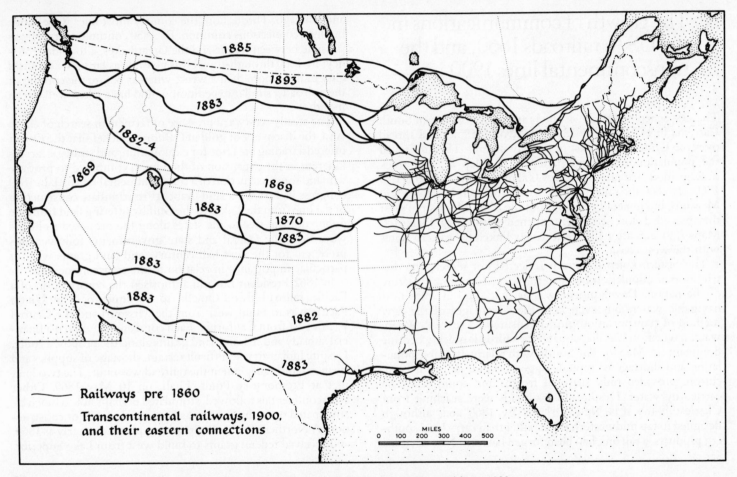

1885

1893

1883

1882-4

1869

1869

1883

1870

1883

1883

1883

1882

1883

—— Railways pre 1860

—— Transcontinental railways, 1900,
and their eastern connections

MILES

0 100 200 300 400 500

10 » Growth of communications in the USA: railroads 1860, and the transcontinental lines 1900

Reaching Bismarck, North Dakota, in 1873 the company went bankrupt, and had to await reorganisation before finally linking with Seattle in 1883. At about the same time the Canadian Pacific was building towards Vancouver, which it reached in 1885. Further south the Kansas Pacific stopped at Denver in 1870, but the Atchison, Topeka and Santa Fé reached the Pacific in 1883; the Denver and Rio Grande provided a connection with the Union Pacific at Ogden (1883), and indirectly via the Oregon lines (1882–4) with the Pacific North-West. Across Texas ran the Texas and Pacific (1882) which joined the Southern Pacific (1883) east of El Paso. Through Montana the Great Northern eventually reached Seattle in 1893.

The building of the seven great transcontinental railroads, although beset by difficulties and shadowed by corruption, opened the West and speeded the closing of the frontier. Exploitation of the mineral and lumber resources of the Rocky Mountains would have been difficult without them, settlement would have been delayed, and the West might have broken its political ties with the East but for the binding power of the rails.

11 The distribution of Negro and foreign-born in the USA, 1790-1900

The two distinctive features of population growth in the United States were, in combination, unique. Accelerating Atlantic migration and the demographic and spatial expansion of the Negro shaped the social structure of the developing nation.

In 1790 the Negro, as a major element in the population, was largely confined to the tidewater South where he had first been introduced as slave labour. Only here were there counties with a majority of Negroes. The Negro population rose from 757,000 in 1790 to 2,329,000 in 1830, despite the abolition of the slave trade in 1808. In 1830 Negroes were still tied to the labour-intensive cotton economy, but the cotton belt had entered its most explosive phase of growth. The development of 'upland' varieties had allowed penetration onto the Piedmont; new areas of production had also been established in southern Alabama, and in Louisiana on the rich bottomlands of the Mississippi and Red Rivers. These areas now lay within the frontier of Negro America. Florida, on the southern frontier, shows high Negro densities in a small total population. In Kentucky the Negro was associated with tobacco cultivation rather than with cotton.

In 1900 the Negro population had reached 8,834,000. Those areas in which Negroes formed at least one in three of the population represent a rural Negro distribution that has remained virtually unchanged (cf. Map 40). Large-scale migration to northern cities did not begin until the First World War, and the traditional equation between the Negro and cotton still generally prevailed. The freeing of the slaves (1863-5) had not freed the Negro from the land. By 1900 the contour of the cotton South had filled out, and a major westward advance had been made into east Texas. In general the Negro followed the crop, but where primitive mechanisation was being introduced the need for labour declined, and cotton outpaced him.

Further north the trans-Atlantic exodus from Europe brought thirty-four million immigrants to the United States in the hundred years from 1820. Their distribution patterns were distinctive, and their choice showed clear ethnic contrast. The index of 20 per cent foreign-born reveals a peripheral pattern for 1900. French-Canadians were prominent in northern Maine and Vermont. The great majority of the Irish and Italians remained in the cities of the manufacturing belt, whereas most of the Germans, Scandinavians and Swiss settled on the farmlands of Wisconsin and Minnesota. Throughout the upper Midwest and the northern plains more than one in five of the population were first-generation Americans. In the Mountain West large numbers of immigrants were attracted by factors as diverse as Mormon recruitment in Europe and the development of the western mining industry. The magnetism of California is also apparent, and the state contained a significant minority of Chinese, many of whom originally entered as sponsored labour to build the transcontinental railroads. In contrast, the high proportion of foreign-born in the south-

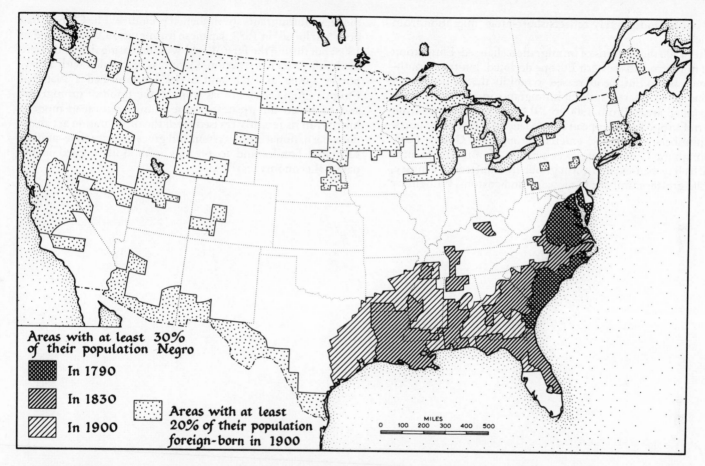

Areas with at least 30%
of their population Negro

In 1790

In 1830

In 1900

Areas with at least
20% of their population
foreign-born in 1900

MILES

0   100 200 300 400 500

11 » The distribution of the Negro population in the USA, 1790 to 1900, and of foreign-born in 1900

west borderlands merely reflects short-range migration from Mexico.

After 1900 the patterns of immigration changed. Emigration from northern and western Europe declined, but from southern and eastern Europe increased so rapidly that 87 per cent of the one-and-a-quarter million immigrants in 1907 came from these 'new' areas. From 1900 to 1914 two million Jews from eastern Europe and European Russia landed at east-coast ports, and numbers of Japanese entered through the Golden Gate. Although the United States was a nation of immigrants, anti-alien feeling had existed throughout the nineteenth century, and the greater number of languages and customs brought by the 'new' immigrants strengthened prejudice. The Chinese had been 'excluded' in 1882; Japanese immigration was checked in 1908; but during the First World War increasing demands were made for general restriction. Congress responded with a temporary quota in 1921, and in 1924 established a National Origins Quota System that stopped the flood of immigrants and so ended the greatest overseas immigration in modern history. In its recently revised form the immigration act abandons the national quota system and gives priority to re-uniting separated familes and to persons with skills needed in the national economy.

12 Population and city growth in the USA, 1790 and 1870

During the first decade after independence there were sharp regional contrasts in population density within the United States. The area of greatest density was the coastal strip from Massachusetts Bay to the Delaware estuary, with a strong salient in the Hudson valley, that contained most of the growing towns and nascent industries. Philadelphia, with a population of 42,520, was still the largest city, although it was soon to be overtaken by New York (33,131). Boston (18,038) was still greater than Baltimore (13,503), but the Massachusetts capital was already beginning to feel the constraints on growth imposed by its restricted hinterland. Although Boston retained considerable commercial and financial importance, its nineteenth-century pre-eminence lay in the cultural sphere.

Charleston (16,359) was the fourth largest town in 1790, but nowhere in the rural South did population density exceed forty-five per square mile. The long-settled tidewater lands around Chesapeake Bay possessed densities of eighteen to forty-five, but these old tobacco lands were already suffering population loss through soil exhaustion. Further south and west population was moving towards the frontier; the Piedmont and the Appalachian valleys already had densities as high as eighteen per square mile, as had the outlier of settlement in Kentucky (cf. Map 8).

By 1870 a much more mature pattern of population distribution appears, reflecting not only regional differences in agricultural productivity, but also widening contrasts in the pace of industrial growth. The United States was still a rural nation; only 21 per cent of the population lived in towns of more than 8,000 inhabitants, although 12 per cent of the population already lived in cities of considerable size. Much the largest was New York which, together with Brooklyn, contained almost 1·4 million people; and since the towns on the New Jersey shore were also growing quickly, Greater New York was clearly being shaped as the nation's major metropolis. Philadelphia (674,000) had been outpaced; Boston (250,000) and Baltimore (267,000) were now smaller than Chicago (300,000) and St Louis (311,000), the regional centres of the Midwest. The growth of these great cities in areas almost empty eighty years earlier is perhaps the most striking feature of Map 12.

Increasingly city development came to shape the growth of the nation and dominated its economic life. The city was the market for the rural farmer and supplied ever wider areas with new techniques and equipment without which neither the farmer nor the city itself could survive and prosper. Despite increasing hostility between the rural and urban elements of American society, both strands were at the same time becoming increasingly interwoven and interdependent.

In the South, New Orleans was the only city of more than 100,000 in 1870, Charleston had now dropped far behind, and in population density as well as in urban growth south and north stood in sharp contrast. Only in South Carolina, Tennessee and Louisiana were there densities of over forty-five per square mile, whereas a zone of this density, and greater, extended from New England to eastern Iowa. In southern

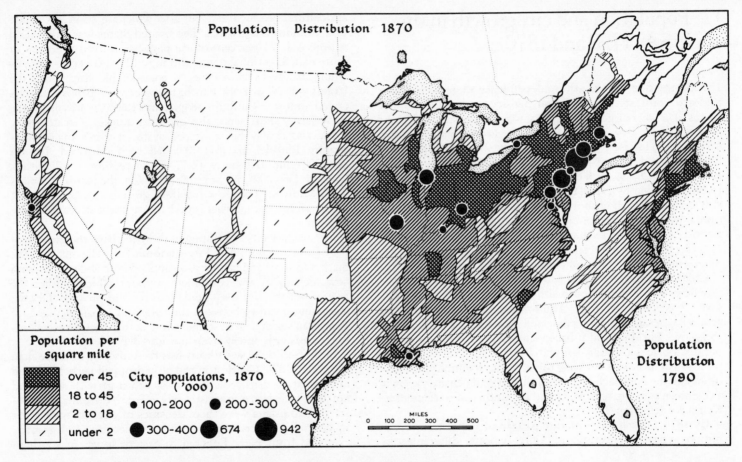

Population Distribution 1870

Population per square mile

- over 45
- 18 to 45
- 2 to 18
- under 2

City populations, 1870 ('000)

- 100-200
- 200-300
- 300-400
- 674
- 942

Population Distribution 1790

MILES
0 100 200 300 400 500

12 » Population and city growth in the USA, 1790 and 1870. *It has not been possible to show the western outliers of settled territory, especially in Kentucky, in 1790; for these see Map 8*

New England, eastern Pennsylvania, and in the Hudson-Mohawk corridor of New York this was increasingly a response to industrialisation; in the rich farmlands of the Midwest high rural population densities reflect the evolution of the Corn Belt as the most productive farm region of the United States (cf. Map 15). Throughout much of the South settlement was still scattered and broken, large areas of forest remained, and population densities were frequently still at the 'post-frontier' level. Map 12 clearly reveals the growth of San Francisco and the development of the rich farmlands of the Pacific Coast.

13 Type-of-farming areas in the USA

Until quite recently the agriculture of the United States was so specialised by region that it was possible to identify broad and relatively simple farming provinces, each dependent on a single dominant crop or product. This classical pattern of major crop belts began to change in the 1920s under the impact of the new agrarian technology; the process was accelerated by the demands of the Second World War and by the changing needs of the post-war period. Map 13, based upon the traditional pattern, incorporates these developments, and shows a more fragmented system of farming areas, each with its own diversity of products and internal structure.

In the heart of North America lies one of the world's most productive agricultural regions, the Corn and Livestock Belt. This area of intensive, highly capitalised and profitable farming yields over one-fifth of the gross value of farm products in the United States. Corn (maize) is everywhere the dominant crop, but is not generally the chief cash crop. Most of the corn is fed as fattening fodder to cattle and pigs, the prosperity of most farmers depending upon sales to the meat-packers. Hay and clover, oats and soya beans are grown in rotation with corn as feedstuffs, and there is a variable proportion of pasture. The land is worked hard, techniques are highly mechanised, and fertilisers are used on a massive scale. Thus an average Corn Belt farm represents a very considerable investment, and agriculture must be both intensive and successful to service a high level of bank loans; partly for this reason large amalgamated 'company farms' run on industrial principles have appeared. However, local variants in farming can be expected in a region that stretches 1,000 miles across the continental heartland. In northern Illinois, in the hinterland of Chicago, corn is grown for cash sale; in south central Illinois, and parts of Indiana and Ohio, soya beans almost equal corn in acreage and are grown both for sale and as feedstuffs. Along the northern boundary of the Corn Belt dairy cattle replace beef cattle, as corn drops out of the rotation in favour of wheat and oats. Corn cannot be grown successfully where summer rainfall is below 8 inches, and in the drier western areas wheat reaches parity with corn; here land use is less intensive, with larger farms, more pasture and a shift of interest from cattle fattening to lean-cattle breeding.

The Dairy Belt, reaching from Maine to Minnesota and straddling the Great Lakes, is a region of less intensive land use; across the 'cutover' wastes of former timber land in northern Michigan and Wisconsin, and in the New England upland, it grades into sterile, uncultivated forest. Throughout the belt summers are cool (65° to 70°F) and winters long and harsh. In New England and the northern Appalachians where agriculture is chiefly confined to the larger river valleys, dairying is partly a response to physical limitations on crop cultivation, but is also related to the relatively high degree of urbanisation. On the glacial deposits of Michigan, Wisconsin and Minnesota dairying is not only a response to the physical environment but also reflects the cultural traditions of the German, Swiss, Scandinavian and Dutch settlers. East of the Great Lakes dairying is chiefly for milk supply to the cities; in the West butter and

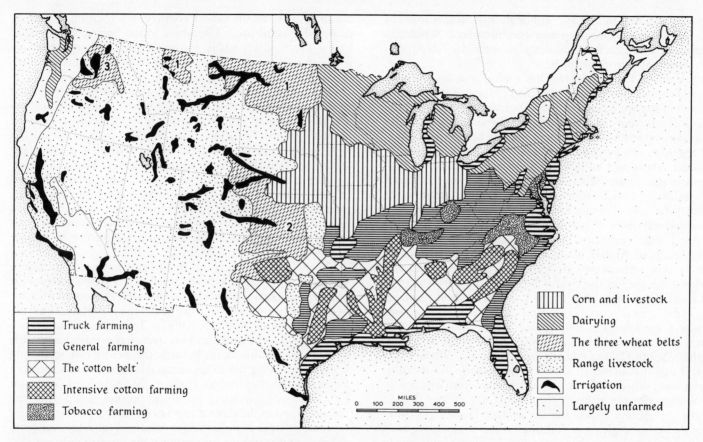

Legend:

Corn and livestock

Dairying

The three 'wheat belts'

Range livestock

Irrigation

Largely unfarmed

Truck farming

General farming

The 'cotton belt'

Intensive cotton farming

Tobacco farming

MILES
0 100 200 300 400 500

13 » Type-of-farming areas in the USA. *The three wheat belts are numbered: 1 = spring wheat; 2 = winter wheat; 3 = the Columbia plateau wheat region*

cheese production dominate, although the 'milk-sheds' of cities like Chicago reach deep into their hinterland. Wisconsin is particularly famous for its domestic cheese and for its American variants of European types.

South of the Corn Belt stretches a long, irregular zone of general farming, once labelled the 'corn and winter wheat belt', for both crops are common. It is a border zone between the agricultural systems of the Midwest and the South, with elements derived from both. Without internal homogeneity, it is best regarded as a patchwork of contrasted farming types. In Missouri wheat and corn, with a strong livestock interest, dominate agriculture. Where the river lands of southern Illinois and Indiana provide soils of great fertility, grain-soya-livestock farming flourishes in the tradition of the Corn Belt, but occasional fields of cotton and tobacco suggest a southern pattern. In total contrast is the rough, half-cultivated country of the southern Appalachians, where subsistence farming of hillbilly type alternates with fruit cultivation, dairying and market gardening in the river valleys. On the north-western and south-western borders of the Corn Belt wheat displaces corn as the most favoured crop. Here lie the two major regions of wheat specialisation, the Spring Wheat and the Winter Wheat Belts, separated by the rough, dry, sand-hill country of southern South Dakota and northern Nebraska. Wheat is the most drought resistant of all the major grains, and its cultivation was pushed westward in the late nineteenth century. In the wheat belts the risks of crop failure are greater than in almost every other region but the average farmer specialises strongly in this single crop. Although wheat is a gamble, most other commercial crops do not produce adequate yields, and in the drier parts of the wheat country any rotation system is completely eliminated. Elsewhere in the Spring Wheat Belt, barley and flax, especially in the Dakotas, are important as rotation crops; in the Winter Wheat Belt sorghum is the chief subordinate crop.

During the past fifty years the Cotton Belt has experienced more radical change than any other region. Classically, cotton was the dominant cash crop throughout the South as far west as north-central Texas but, since the 1920s, cotton acreage has been halved. The Cotton Belt became fragmented as acreage contracted into the most favoured areas (cf. Map 17). Cultivation is almost completely mechanised, with the introduction of sophisticated machinery replacing the enormous amount of hand labour that traditional cotton farming demanded. This belated technical revolution is associated with the reappearance of the large farm, almost a neo-plantation, similar to the 'company farms' of the Corn Belt.

On the immense acreage freed from cotton cultivation a variety of new crops has been introduced. Early vegetables for northern markets are widely grown along the coastal margins of the old Cotton Belt. Near the growing cities of the South are large dairy herds and, especially in Texas, large numbers of beef cattle. Special crops and products have proved adaptable to southern conditions, for example the 'peanut belt' stretching from coastal Virginia to southern Alabama, and the poultry farms of northern Georgia. In short, the South has worked out its agricultural salvation by diversification. Long after the emancipation of the slave it remained in slavery to cotton; not until the collapse of the cotton economy in the inter-war years did the region seize the opportunity for agrarian progress that had eluded it for so long.

Truck farming (market gardening) does not dominate a single region but occurs in a number of smaller areas particularly favoured by mild climates and suitable soils. Proximity to urban markets is also a relevant factor, and the coastal strip from Cape Cod to Virginia, now called 'Megalopolis', has an urban market of over forty million people. Transportation developments have, however, reduced the importance of close association with metropolitan centres, and Florida and the Gulf South produce not only early vegetables but also tropical products such as sugar cane, rice and citrus fruits. Fruit and vegetables also dominate the irrigated valleys and southern coastal lowlands of California.

More than a third of the total area of the United States lies within the Western Range livestock region, extending from the semi-arid margins of crop cultivation on the Great Plains to the Pacific mountains. The chief agricultural resource of this region is dry grassland, much of it still in public ownership (cf. Map 48), that degenerates into scrub and semi-desert in the most arid areas. This poor grazing is only suitable for short seasonal use, and a complex system of seasonal migration, once by cattle drives, now by truck, is characteristic of the western cattle industry. The principal economic function of the Western Range is the production of lean stock for 'export' shipment eastwards to the fattening farms of the Corn Belt, although the development of irrigation farming is gradually changing this pattern. The Platte, the Snake and the Missouri provide irrigation water for ribbons of fertile and intensively worked cropland; these interrupt the parched pastures of the west and provide high-value feed, especially alfalfa, that makes possible the local fattening of beef stock.

14 Type-of-farming areas in Canada

The Prairie Provinces dominate Canada's agricultural profile. Centred on the Chernozem soils of Saskatchewan is a zone of highly mechanised wheat farming, with little livestock interest and only a small acreage of other grains. On the drier south-western plains, beef cattle replace wheat, and this area of poor pasture is an extension of the United States range-cattle region. Concentrations of beef cattle are also found on the Alberta foothills of the Rocky Mountains, and in the moister areas of Manitoba. Along the northern margins of the wheat belt lies a broad zone of mixed farming which degenerates to semi-pioneering against the forest fringe but extends a salient to the Peace River country, the ultimate northern limit of prairie agriculture. North-east and south-east of the specialised wheat belt are other districts of more general farming, where wheat is important but not dominant.

In the Mountain West agriculture is restricted by relief. Important orchards of apples, peaches and apricots are found around Lakes Okanagan and Kootenay in the warmer southern parts of British Columbia; beef and dairy cattle are reared in the interior valleys around Kamloops, but most intensive dairying is found in the immediate hinterland of Vancouver.

Agriculture in the Maritime Provinces and in Quebec is similarly restricted to narrow ribbons and islands of glacial and alluvial soil, and to coastal strips enjoying milder climates and longer growing seasons. Woods and pasture dominate, crop-land is devoted to hay and oats, and livestock products contribute the chief source of cash income. In favoured parts of Nova Scotia and New Brunswick more intensive and specialised cropping occurs: potatoes are an important cash crop in Prince Edward Island and New Brunswick, and the Annapolis valley of Nova Scotia is renowned for its apples. The agricultural heartland of Quebec is the St Lawrence valley where intensive dairy farming is practised side by side with vegetable and fruit cultivation. Penetrating the forests of the Shield is a zone of general farming on the clay belt, and deep within the northern forests, on glacial drift and old lake-beds, are pockets of agriculture serving isolated mining, smelting and paper-pulp towns.

In Ontario, intensive dairying along the St Lawrence is continued locally along the shores of Lakes Ontario and Erie, but these rich terrace soils are also used for intensive vegetable production and, in Norfolk county, for tobacco. The Niagara scarp is orchard covered. Close to Windsor, Ontario, corn and livestock farming of Corn Belt type is prevalent. North of this favoured agricultural region focussed on the Great Lakes, farming becomes more sporadic.

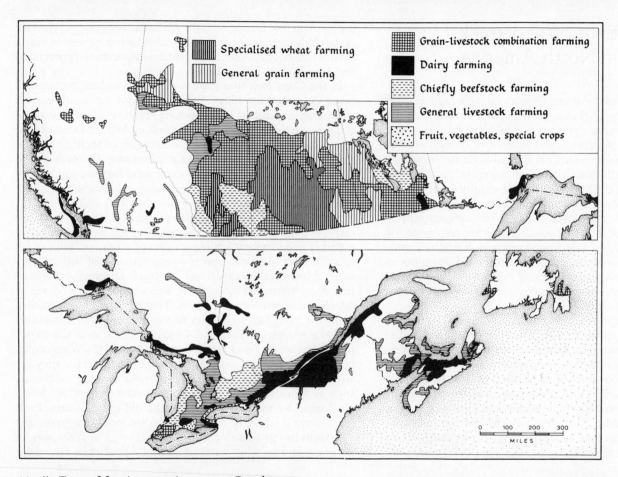

Legend:

- Specialised wheat farming
- General grain farming
- Grain-livestock combination farming
- Dairy farming
- Chiefly beefstock farming
- General livestock farming
- Fruit, vegetables, special crops

0   100   200   300
MILES

14a » Type-of-farming areas in western Canada
14b » Type-of-farming areas in eastern Canada

15 Corn cultivation and 'truck farming' in North America

Corn, or maize, is North America's most valuable crop. East of a line from Montana to Texas corn is grown almost everywhere on a commercial scale, except in New England, and northern Michigan, Wisconsin and Minnesota, though even in these areas it is still cultivated on a small scale for local and road-side sale. Within this vast region of general distribution lies the Corn Belt of the Midwest. On the magnificently fertile prairie soils cultivation is intensive and yields, especially for hybrid varieties, are very high. By 1975 the national output peaked at 6·2 billion bushels, necessitating the extension of stockpiles in the face of a decline in effective world demand. This fact, together with the effects of prolonged droughts in 1976 and 1977, means that stockpiling may take on an increasingly crucial role in the Midwest's economy as a way of balancing surplus and deficit.

The western margin of corn cultivation is dictated by declining rainfall, which reduces yields below commercially viable limits. Beyond the drought barrier cultivation is only possible on irrigated land, as in the Mormon settlements of Utah. Until the 1930s the northern limit of the Corn Belt was the climatic limit of the plant itself, which required a mean temperature of 65° to 75°F for the three summer months and a growing season of 120 to 140 days. More recently, hybridisation has produced short-season varieties better adapted to the cooler north. Corn now occupies an increased acreage in the 'dairy belt', emphasising its main role throughout the Midwest as an essential fodder crop. Although summer rainfall of 8 inches or less is still a barrier to intensive cultivation, corn is now a secondary crop in the drier Spring Wheat Belt.

In the Corn Belt it is grown mainly as fodder, sometimes being cut green for silage, but throughout the South corn is cultivated for human consumption. Traditionally corn was the staple foodstuff of the southern small-holder, both black and white, but changes in agriculture have played their part in the slowly transforming patterns of southern life. Throughout the old Cotton Belt beef and dairy cattle have increased in importance, stimulating local but large-scale and highly intensive corn production for fodder, almost on Corn Belt lines.

Fruit, nut and vegetable production, although in many respects quite different branches of farming, are here grouped together because they represent types of intensive land use for specialised crops, with specific requirements of soil and climate. Most market gardening, or truck farming, is concentrated on fertile terraces along the coastal plains, close to developed urban concentrations. The urbanised north-eastern seaboard from Massachusetts to Virginia, and the shorelands of Lake Michigan, Erie and Ontario, are among the major producing areas. Truck farmers in Florida and California compete in these markets with early fruit and vegetables; they are also large producers for the freezing and canning industries, such as Florida orange juice, but are now themselves being challenged by the new centres in the old cotton states. Fruit crops have a strongly localised distribution. Temperate and soft fruits are grown in the 'apple valleys' of Washington, in Virginia, and in other parts of central Appalachia, famed for

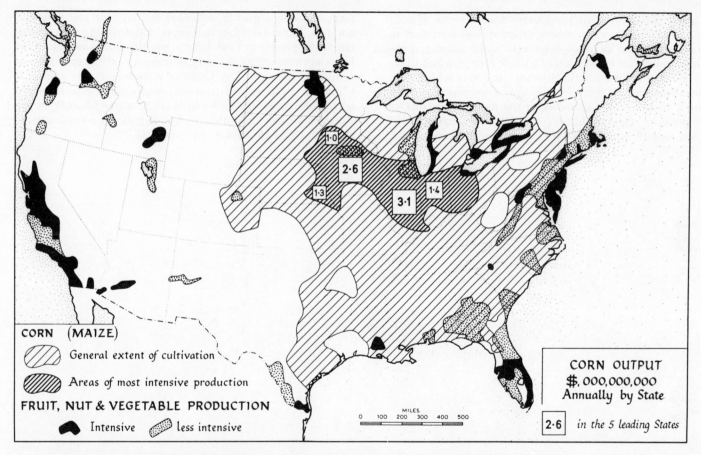

CORN (MAIZE)

General extent of cultivation

Areas of most intensive production

FRUIT, NUT & VEGETABLE PRODUCTION

Intensive   less intensive

MILES
0 100 200 300 400 500

CORN OUTPUT
$, 000,000,000
Annually by State

2·6   in the 5 leading States

15 » Corn cultivation and fruit, nut and vegetable production in North America. *Values are given for production in each of the five leading states, 1975 preliminary figures*

local cider. In citrus fruit production south-central Florida rivals southern California, where urban sprawl continues to reduce the acreage of orange groves. Some districts have developed intensive cultivation of a single crop; the Red River valley of North Dakota and Minnesota, together with south-eastern Idaho and northern Maine, specialises in potato cultivation; a small area in Louisiana is the national supplier of sweet potatoes. Georgia has recently become famous for its peanuts, though within a wider agricultural transformation, responding to a greatly increased demand for vegetable oils and fats. Extensive vineyards support flourishing wine industries in upper New York state along the shores of Lake Erie, but vineyards are particularly dominant in the Napa valley of central California. The Ontario peninsula is the centre of Canadian apple and soft-fruit cultivation, although other areas, such as the Annapolis valley in Nova Scotia and the Okanogan valley of British Columbia, make a significant contribution to this branch of agriculture (cf. Map 14).

16 Wheat and tobacco cultivation in North America

Except in the arid lands of the West wheat can be grown, and in the past was grown, almost everywhere in the United States and southern Canada. However, as wheat is the most drought tolerant of the major food crops, cultivation has been pushed progressively westward. In the East it has now been largely replaced by other crops, and only occupies a minor role in the rotation system. Despite the risk of drought the wheat belts of contemporary North America are well suited to cultivation of the crop: the level plains of Chernozem and Chestnut soils permit highly mechanised farming, and although yield per acre is relatively low it is high per man employed. In the past wheat cultivation was a conscious gamble against two risks: the prospect of drought and the vagaries of prices on the wheat exchange. In the inter-war years income in the wheat belts varied enormously from year to year as the gamble either failed or succeeded. Today, price supports have reduced one risk, and the abandonment of submarginal land, together with the use of deep-well irrigation, has helped to minimise the climatic hazard. Nevertheless, a strong speculative element remains.

The largest of the three chief concentrations of wheat cultivation is the Spring Wheat Belt, straddling the 49th parallel. Harsh winters prevent autumn sowing, and the critical factors are the length of the growing season and the amount of rainfall. In the Canadian Prairies wheat extends into the dry south-western section of Saskatchewan, which has only 12 inches of rainfall, and also into areas along the northern margins with only 100 frost-free days, but yields in these regions are low and uncertain. The main zone of Spring Wheat stretches from central Saskatchewan across the Dakotas. Further south is the Winter Wheat Belt of Kansas and Oklahoma, where winters are mild enough for autumn-sown wheat to survive, but greater evaporation means that the minimum rainfall for successful cultivation is about 18 inches. The Columbia Plateau Wheat Belt occupies the only part of the intermontane plateaux with rainfall high enough for cropping without irrigation; although only about 15 inches in the shadow of the Cascades, it reaches 20 inches to 30 inches in the eastern areas of the belt. Yields, which are partly a reflection of rainfall, are generally twice as high as in the other wheat regions.

Tobacco cultivation was the great staple of the tidewater lands of colonial Virginia. By the eighteenth century these were exhausted and tobacco spread to the 'Old Belt' of inner Virginia. Today there are essentially two dominant areas, one stretching from southern Virginia through the Carolinas to Georgia, the other in Kentucky and Tennessee. The quality of the leaf is determined by soil type and by the curing process. The heavy soils of the 'Old Belt' produce dark tobaccos whilst from the sandy soils further south comes lighter leaf. Flue curing produces a tobacco suitable for cigarette manufacture; fire curing results in a darker product. Air-cured tobaccos grown in Kentucky were once favoured for pipe smoking, but an increasing proportion are now blended into cigarettes.

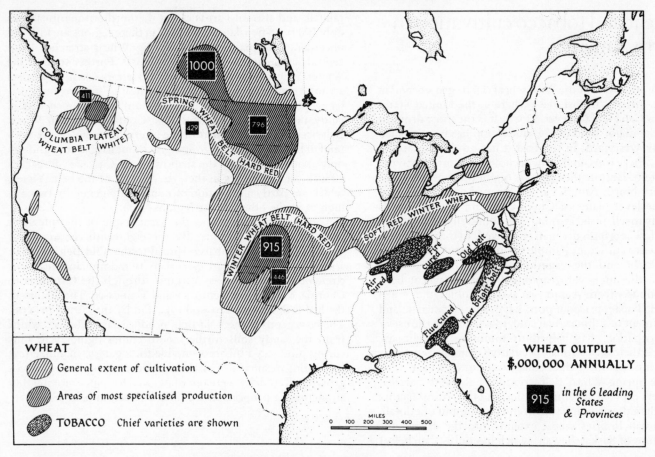

WHEAT

1000

411

429

796

SPRING WHEAT BELT (HARD RED)

COLUMBIA PLATEAU
WHEAT BELT (WHITE)

WINTER WHEAT BELT (HARD RED)

915

446

SOFT RED WINTER WHEAT

Air
cured

Fire
cured

Old belt

Flue cured

New bright belt

TOBACCO

WHEAT

▨ General extent of cultivation

▨ Areas of most specialised production

▨ TOBACCO Chief varieties are shown

**WHEAT OUTPUT
$,000,000 ANNUALLY**

915 *in the 6 leading
States
& Provinces*

MILES
0 100 200 300 400 500

16 » Wheat and tobacco cultivation in North America. *Values are given for production in each of the six
leading states and provinces, 1976 preliminary figures*

17 Oats and cotton cultivation in North America

Oats are not one of North America's major or most valuable crops: there is no conventional 'oat belt', and the crop plays a subordinate and decreasing role in rotation systems. It is grown around the St Lawrence, the southern Great Lakes and from Pennsylvania across the Midwest into the Canadian prairies where it has been a significant element in the zone of general, semi-pioneering farming along the northern margins of the Prairie Provinces.

The cultivation of oats is traditionally associated with dairying, particularly in Minnesota and Wisconsin, providing good straw and silage. In the Corn Belt oats are chiefly used as additional fodder. For human consumption oats are processed mainly for breakfast foods. In the droughts of the mid-1970s oat cultivation was further reduced, with farmers preferring to concentrate upon more valuable crops such as corn and sorghums. Although steady decline in acreage has been associated with yield increases, nevertheless oat cultivation now plays a fairly minor role in the overall agricultural economy.

Cotton cultivation too has changed in response to a series of wider natural and market developments. With the demand for cotton growing rapidly in the industrial revolution, cotton spread far beyond its American beginnings on the 'Sea Islands' off the Carolinas and Georgia, expanding to the climatic limits of cultivation. It needs at least 200 frost-free days and a mean summer temperature of at least 77°F, and these critical requirements set the northern boundary of the crop; to the west its advance was halted by aridity. Apart from later extensions onto the plains of Oklahoma and Texas these limits had been reached by the Civil War. Expansion of cotton cultivation was, however, quickly followed by contraction. The boll-weevil, soil erosion, over-production and declining prices brought a crisis to the Cotton Belt in the 1920s and 1930s. Today cotton has been abandoned as a staple throughout much of the South, although remaining strongly as part of a diversified agricultural base. Production is concentrated in a few clearly defined districts: the inner Coast Plain and Piedmont of Georgia and the Carolinas, northern Alabama, the lower Mississippi valley, the black waxy prairies of central Texas and the high plains of Oklahoma and western Texas. Texas now leads in cotton production, partly due to irrigation that permits its expansion beyond the traditional climatic limits. Further west cotton forms a dominant crop in the irrigated valleys of the Rio Grande in New Mexico, the Gila in Arizona and the San Joaquin in California. The last of these now produces more cotton than any of the old cotton states, and western cotton would have increased further but for federal price supports and acreage allotments that maintain substandard producers in the more traditional areas.

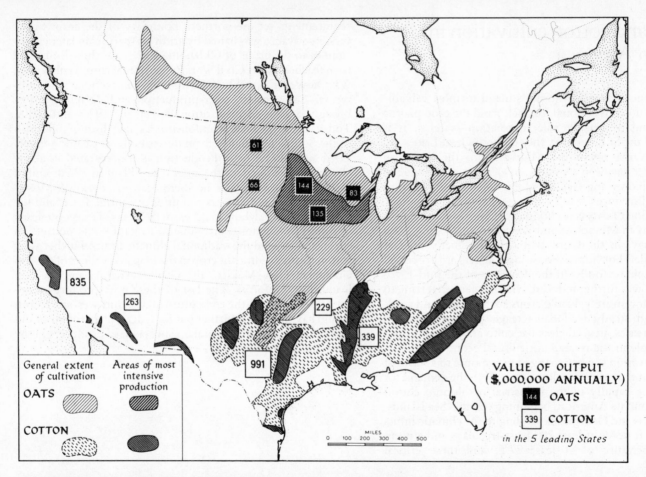

VALUE OF OUTPUT ($,000,000 ANNUALLY)

144 OATS
339 COTTON

in the 5 leading States

General extent of cultivation | Areas of most intensive production

OATS

COTTON

MILES
0 100 200 300 400 500

61
66
144
83
135
835
263
229
339
991

17 » Oats and cotton cultivation in North America. *Values are given for production in each of the five leading states, 1976 preliminary figures*

18 The distribution of sheep and hogs in North America

Sheep rearing and pig keeping occupy completely different sectors in the geography of livestock farming in North America. Sheep are widespread across the semi-arid grazing lands of the western ranges, where they compete with cattle, usually unsuccessfully except on the poorest land. They dominate the cooler grasslands of the northern states, and also the highest and roughest range, with areas of local prominence in Colorado and California. The greatest concentrations of sheep are to be found on the driest rangeland, such as the Llano Estacado of Texas. In the past, western sheep were reared both for wool and for mutton, but wool consumption has slumped in competition with man-made fibres and fat-lamb production has been found to have greater growth potential. This change has been facilitated by the availability of rich fodder produced on western irrigated land, and fat-lamb production on a localised but considerable scale is now found in California, Utah, Colorado and Nebraska. Compared to the overwhelming market preference for beef, fat-lamb production caters nationally only to a limited, minority taste.

Hogs are much more important to the farm economy and are one of the chief cash products of the Corn Belt. They are the dominant animal over much of the region, particularly in Iowa and Illinois, and are the main raw material of the meat-packing industries. A comparison of Maps 15 and 18 will show the close correlation between the distribution of hogs and the limits of the area of corn production. The two districts of most intensive hog production roughly outline the Corn Belt, where hogs are the main consumers of corn. In the gap between these two districts, in central Illinois, both corn and soya beans are grown for direct sale, and hogs are fewer. From the Corn Belt they spread in two directions: they are reared throughout the greater part of the Dairy Belt as subsidiary enterprises, especially in the butter and cheese areas where they are fed on skimmed milk; similarly, production extends across the belt of dairy and general farming north of the wheat region of the Canadian Prairies. In the southern states hogs are reared almost everywhere, but not on an intensive scale. Typically the tenant farmer or share cropper raises them at subsistence level, just as he grows an acre or two of corn for his own food supply. However, the southern agricultural revolution has affected this branch of agriculture as most others, and in those parts of the South where fodder crops have displaced cotton, for example in southern Georgia, hogs are now being reared on a commercial scale.

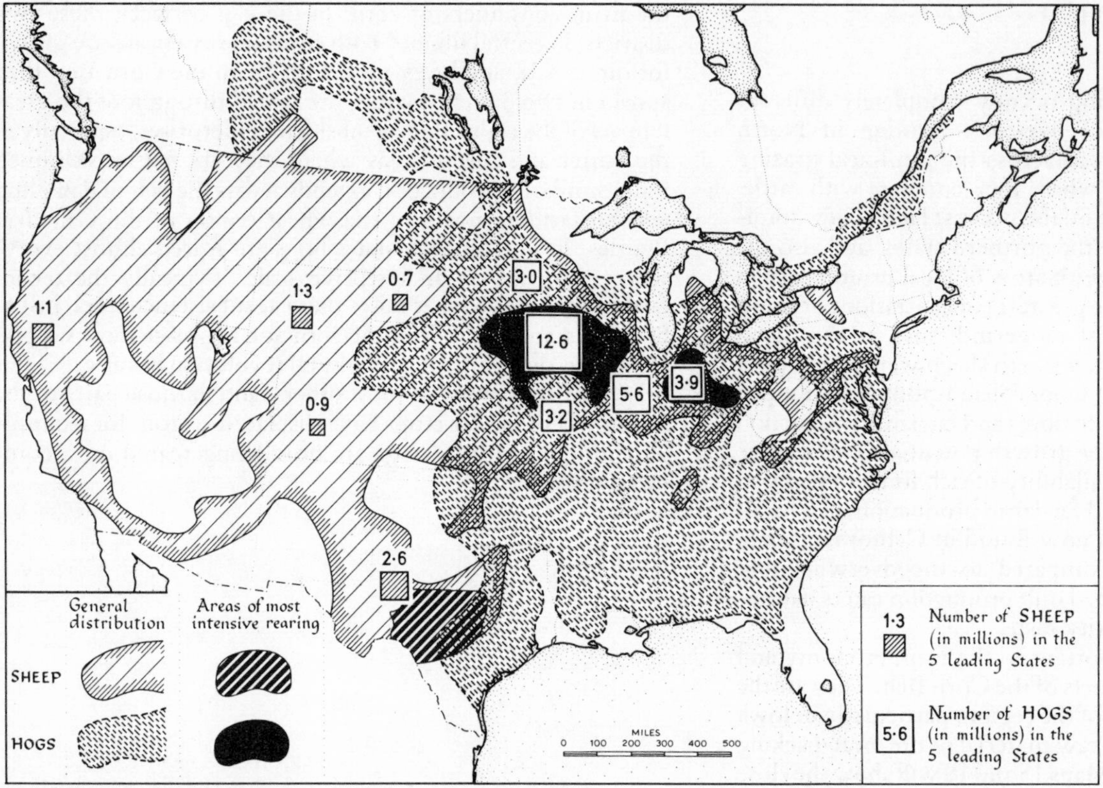

1·1
1·3
0·7
3·0
12·6
5·6
3·9
3·2
0·9
2·6
General distribution
Areas of most intensive rearing
SHEEP
HOGS
MILES
0 100 200 300 400 500
1·3
Number of SHEEP (in millions) in the 5 leading States
5·6
Number of HOGS (in millions) in the 5 leading States

18 » The distribution of sheep and hogs in North America. *Numbers are given for each of the five leading states, 1976 preliminary figures*

19 The distribution of dairy and beef cattle in North America

The geography of cattle rearing is increasingly complex. Factors influencing dairy and beef cattle vary, reflecting different market forces. Dairy cattle are most important between the upper Midwest and New England, extending northwards along the valley of the St Lawrence. The leading dairy producers are Wisconsin and Minnesota, concentrating upon cheese and related products, and the supply of fresh milk is left to those areas surrounding the major population centres, such as upstate New York. Dairying is, however, practised on a less intensive scale across wide areas of the United States and Canada, and is the dominant theme of farming against the forest fringe of the Prairie Provinces. In the far West small centres in the valleys of southern California almost rival Wisconsin in intensity. In such disparate areas as Michigan and Alabama the numbers of milch cows have been dramatically reduced, but this has been offset by increased efficiency to maintain approximately the same position in terms of farm sales as in 1945.

Until the 1950s the distribution of beef cattle in the United States followed a simple regional pattern. Lean cattle were reared on the dry ranges of the West, and shipped east to the Corn Belt for fattening. This movement continues, but with greater complexity. The explosive growth of California has led to large-scale fattening within the state, from fodder grown on irrigated land, and most of the lean cattle from the south-western states now go west rather than north and east for fattening. In addition, throughout much of the semi-arid western range, irrigation schemes allow local fattening of some lean stock. One of the greatest recent changes in the geography of beef production has been the emergence of the South. New cross-breeds have been developed, better able to withstand the hot, humid climate, and land once devoted to cotton has been put to the production of fodder. Texan cattle are now fattened within the state, and parts of Mississippi and Florida have concentrations of cattle reminiscent of the Corn Belt. The greatest transformation has occurred in the 'black belt' of Alabama; in this district of fertile prairie soils, beef and dairy cattle form important elements in a diversified farming system that has replaced the old cotton-based agrarian economy. Large herds graze the lands once worked by slaves and exhausted by cotton, now restored with improved grasses and intensive fertilisation, and make a significant contribution to the new prosperity of much of the South.

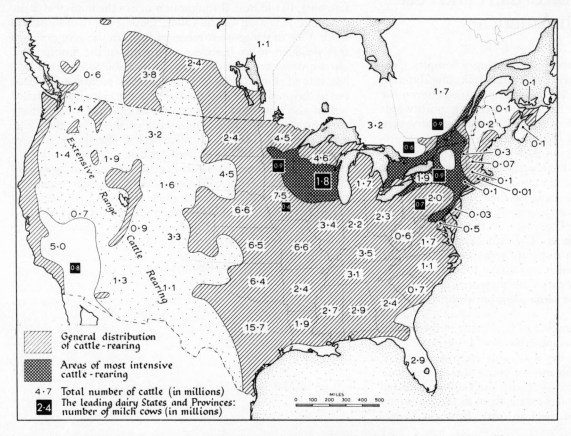

General distribution of cattle-rearing

Areas of most intensive cattle-rearing

4·7 Total number of cattle (in millions)

2·4 The leading dairy States and Provinces: number of milch cows (in millions)

MILES
0 100 200 300 400 500

19 » The distribution of cattle in North America. *Numbers are given for all types of cattle, and for milch cows in the eight leading dairy states and provinces, 1976 preliminary figures*

20 The coal resources of North America

The Industrial Revolution was built upon coal. North America's black gold drove pistons, fired boilers, heated the homes and fouled the air. After the boom of the 1940s coal increasingly lost its markets to clean and seemingly ever-abundant oil. Now, however, oil production is declining and the United States' economy is dangerously dependent upon foreign supplies. Proven gas reserves are dwindling and nuclear power faces an uncertain future. Domestic coal resources however are superabundant, a 340-year supply at current levels of demand. However, by the early 1960s coal production had slumped from a wartime high of over 600 million tons to about 400 million tons, some 23 per cent of the total fuel consumed. By 1975 production reached a new peak of 640 million tons, though representing a very different pattern of supply, and President Carter has indicated a target of 1,200 million tons a year by 1985.

Traditionally American coal came largely from three active areas: the anthracite of eastern Pennsylvania, the bituminous coal of the Appalachians, and the eastern interior field of Illinois, Indiana and western Kentucky. The first of these, though small, has been intensively worked. Despite the high cost of recovery from thin and steeply pitching seams, anthracite was the standard domestic fuel until competition from oil and natural gas and the partial exhaustion of its reserves brought the industry close to extinction, with massive unemployment in the Wilkes-Barre area.

Though America's usable reserves are split equally between East and West the major area of production remains the Appalachians. The 'Pittsburgh bed' coking coals are now exhausted, and the focus has shifted south into West Virginia where seams have traditionally been thick and easily worked from deep mines. Fifteen major companies are responsible for over 60 per cent of the field's production, and increasingly extract coal by capital-intensive, surface techniques, particularly in the western part of the field reaching into Ohio. Opencast mining, favoured for its ease of mechanisation and low manpower needs, now accounts for half the bituminous output. Coal from this area supplies the needs of the Middle Atlantic states, particularly the power stations.

The Illinois-based eastern interior field came to supply the Midwest increasingly from opencast workings. Unfortunately much of this is high in sulphur and so was declared unusable by the 1970 Clean Air Act. The search for an inexpensive, domestic and sulphur-free coal source has turned attention to the West. From New Mexico to Alberta output has traditionally been slight, producing for local power stations and the West's scattered iron and steel works. Thick, local low-sulphur seams and ease of open-cast access have stimulated much activity, with all the associated environmental problems of these fragile, often desert areas. With eastern mining being more labour intensive, subject to irregular supply through wildcat strikes against the safety hazards, and being restricted by its high sulphur content, the potential for further development would seem to lie in the West if the United States is indeed to reach energy independence. The environmental costs however could be high, whether in devastation or in reclamation costs to be passed on to fuel-hungry consumers if the 1977 Surface Mining Control and Reclamation Act is made effective.

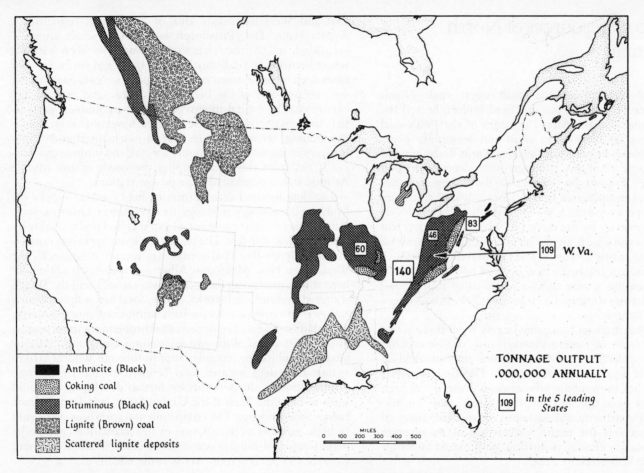

Legend:

- ■ **Anthracite (Black)**
- ░ **Coking coal**
- ▓ **Bituminous (Black) coal**
- ▒ **Lignite (Brown) coal**
- ▒ **Scattered lignite deposits**

TONNAGE OUTPUT
.000,000 ANNUALLY

109 *in the 5 leading States*

83 46 60 140 109 W. Va.

20 » The coal resources of North America. *Tonnage output of bituminous and coking coals is given for each of the five leading states, 1975 figures*

21 Natural gas and gas pipelines in North America

The rise of natural gas to the status of a major fuel has been one of the most remarkable developments in the recent economic history of North America. Almost ignored before the 1920s and usually burned off as waste, by 1940 gas supplied 11 per cent of the energy requirements of the USA, and in the 1960s almost reached parity with oil. It is a direct competitor however with coal, rather than oil, competing in the same markets and for similar purposes: 34 per cent of gas production goes to domestic consumers for heating, over 51 per cent to industrial users. Its convenience and high calorific value make it an ideal fuel, and during the 1960s coal output declined as that of gas rose. By the mid-1970s natural gas provided over half the fuel used both for domestic and commercial heating and for industrial purposes.

The great markets for natural gas are the urban centres of the manufacturing belt, in contrast to the major sources, which lie in the south-central states and in Alaska where industrial and domestic demands, though increasing, are still limited. A complex pipeline system has therefore been necessary to link production areas with the national market. Large-scale investment has resulted in a network of almost 700,000 miles of gas pipeline in the USA, compared to only about 200,000 miles of railroad. A further 4,000 miles of pipeline have been approved to bring North Slope Alaskan gas south through Canada and on to both California and the Midwest.

Canada too has exploited its gas reserves. Extensive fields have been developed in the prairies, particularly Alberta, with a northern outlier in the Peace River country. These are connected by pipeline with the major Canadian cities and manufacturing areas. Recent finds include the potentially massive Mackenzie Bay field in the northern Yukon west of the American Prudhoe Bay field. Much Canadian gas is pumped south to the United States, though frequently this is resented by Canadian consumers, particularly in the eastern cities.

Most oilfields produce natural gas, but it is of only local significance. The three major Appalachian producers, Kentucky, Pennsylvania and West Virginia, together produce less than 2 per cent of the total output, but the Ontario field is important as a domestic source for Canadian industry. There is significant production from the mountain states, particularly Wyoming, and also from California, Kansas, and the prairie fields of Alberta, but the natural gas fields of Texas and Louisiana are utterly dominant. They supply three-quarters of total output; adding the contribution of adjacent states, almost 90 per cent of total production comes from this south-central region. Newly exploited reserves in the Tuscaloosa Sand of southern Louisiana have added to the region's dominance, and exploration of the geopressured zones off the Gulf Coast suggests the possibility of production rising to two trillion cubic feet a year by the end of the century, or 10 per cent of the present US national consumption. Some consumers outside these producing states have however been cut off or had supplies curtailed. Since 1954 the Federal Power Commission has regulated the well-head price of gas involved in interstate commerce, keeping the cost to the industrial heartland down

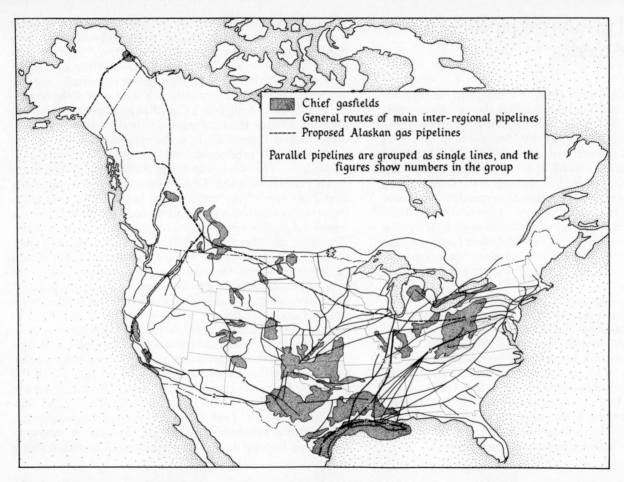

21 » Natural gas in North America

but discouraging further commercial development except to supply markets within the producer states.

Elaborate pipeline systems deliver the gas to distant markets, and Map 21 traces a generalised summary of their complexity. Several pipes connect the Hugoten-Panhandle field that straddles Kansas, Oklahoma and north-west Texas with the Chicago market. From the richer Monroe and Gulf Coast fields of Texas and Louisiana a pipeline corridor follows the Mississippi valley to supply the Midwest. A complex of five pipes leads across Kentucky to serve the urbanised North-East. Another major pipeline, built during the Second World War to carry oil, follows the Coastal Plain route to the seaboard cities.

From the Mountain West natural gas is carried to Oregon and Washington, but supplies for the west coast come mainly from two widely separated areas. Southern California draws from the Permian Basin field of west Texas, while northern California and the Pacific Northwest are supplied from the Alberta and the Peace River fields of Canada. Increasingly under competition from electricity outside the production areas, and with producers looking to unregulated local demand in the burgeoning 'sunbelt' (cf Map 38), both the production and the distribution of natural gas may come to involve retrenchment. Even the arrival of Alaska supplies due in 1983 will only alleviate the long-term uncertainty of natural-gas supplies. The proven reserves of the Prudhoe Bay field, 26 trillion cubic feet, are only sufficient to meet the current total demand for one year.

22 Oil production and refining in the USA

The United States is rich in oil, but increasingly people are being forced to realise that this is an ephemeral resource. The progressive depletion of known reserves has paralleled the increase in consumer demand. Despite the fuel shortage of 1974 demand continues to rise and has been met primarily by increased imports from the Middle East. The tripling of the well-head price for oil has encouraged not only further exploration within the United States, but, more significantly, has permitted the economic exploitation of once prohibitively expensive domestic supplies, such as those at Prudhoe Bay on the Alaskan Arctic coast. Massive, partly foreign, investment has been necessary for the Alaskan supplies to be piped south to the Pacific coast for shipment to the lower forty-eight states. Despite environmentalists' objections, construction was finally authorised and oil moving south by 1977. As North America has been exhaustively prospected no further major fields are anticipated though further price rises could well permit once unprofitable fields to be opened or re-opened. Hopefully limited future oil reserves will be used primarily where there are no possible substitutes, such as for certain types of lubrication, rather than where feasible substitutes do exist, as for power stations.

Many of the fields, such as those in western Pennsylvania where oil was first drilled in 1859, are now insignificant relict producers. The fields of the Midwest provide small amounts for local consumption only. The southern Illinois field illustrates the fluctuations and uncertainties of the industry. A major producer between 1900 and 1920, it became exhausted and was largely abandoned in the 1930s. Later in that decade deep drilling techniques were introduced, and there was a tenfold increase in output to approximately 6 per cent of the national total. In the 1940s production again declined, but after 1954 the introduction of 'water flood' operations once again raised output to some 4 per cent of national production. By 1974 production was down to below 1 per cent.

The large and scattered fields of the Rocky Mountains and the Great Plains have also had a chequered history as the pattern of production has shifted with decline and new discovery. Wyoming has long been the richest producer, with 4 per cent of national output. With the spectacular rise in world oil prices the vast shale oil deposits of the Rockies, particularly in Colorado, are now under examination, though the technological processes involved in releasing the oil may make the extraction environmentally devastating to an unacceptable scale. The once rich fields of California's San Joaquin valley and Los Angeles lowlands have been overworked and so their share of national output has declined from 17 per cent to 10 per cent over the last thirty years. California has become a net importer of oil and, with the arrival of Alaskan oil, supplies seem adequate for some years to come.

The greatest reserves now lie in the Gulf Coast, Midcontinental, and Alaskan fields. These are also the largest producers, from which oil pipelines radiate to supply the national market: Texas supplies California and parts of the Midwest; the bulk of petroleum products from Kansas and Oklahoma go to the

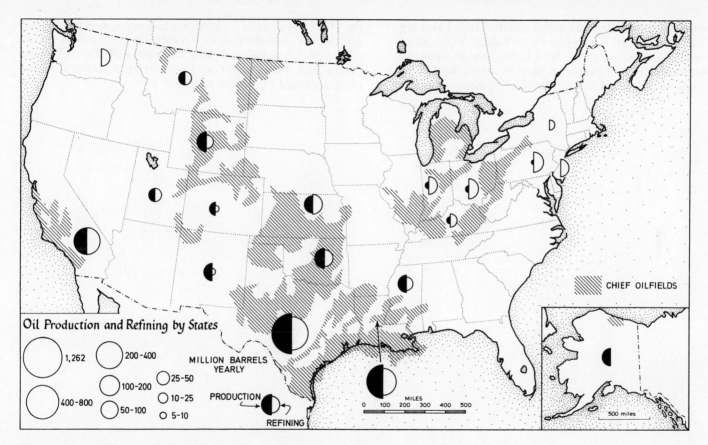

Oil Production and Refining by States

MILLION BARRELS YEARLY

1,262
400-800
200-400
100-200
50-100
25-50
10-25
5-10

PRODUCTION
REFINING

CHIEF OILFIELDS

MILES
0   100   200   300   400   500

500 miles

22 » Oil production and refining in the USA, 1974 preliminary figures

industrial centres of the Ohio valley and the Great Lakes region; and Alaska's oil is shipped from Valdez, the southern terminal of the pipeline, to the West Coast, though some may become earmarked for export to Japan to relieve the US balance of payments deficit. Despite the development of pipelines the Mississippi retains a significant role in conveying crude oil and refined products into the continental heartland by barge. Although Louisiana is linked by pipe with the urbanised North-East, the bulk of Gulf Coast 'exports' to the seaboard cities is carried by coastal tanker.

23 Hydrocarbons and non-ferrous metals in Canada

One of the great changes in the geography of energy supplies in North America since 1945 has been the discovery and development of immense new resources of both oil and natural gas in the Prairie Provinces of Canada. Previously, the Dominion's only satisfactory energy base was its well-developed hydro-electricity (cf. Map 24). Small quantities of coal were produced from the difficult fields of the Maritimes and from the then poorly exploited deposits of the Prairies (cf. Map 20), but the bulk of consumption was imported from the United States. An era of massive exploration and development has transformed Canada's energy budget. Today the country is a major exporter of both oil and natural gas to the United States. Cheap indigenous oil and natural gas have stimulated industrial growth, and the balance of payments position with the United States has been improved.

Neither oil nor gas are new to the Prairies. Gas has been known since 1885, while the little Turner Valley oilfield near Calgary was opened in 1925. During the Second World War the remote Norman Wells oilfield on the Mackenzie enjoyed a certain strategic significance. The tar sands, a large oil resource near Lake Athabasca, were also known but worked only experimentally. With the rise in the world price for oil this 300,000 million barrel reserve may become commercially and technologically feasible. Major exploitation of hydrocarbons in the Prairie Provinces, however, did not begin until 1947,

with the opening of the Leduc field near Edmonton. The Redwater and Lloydminster fields followed, and by the mid-1950s it was evident that oilfields on a massive scale existed throughout southern Alberta and extended into south-western Saskatchewan. Later still, large resources were found straddling the Saskatchewan-Manitoba boundary, on the north flank of the Williston Basin. Although the search was primarily for oil, many promising structures proved to be richer in natural gas, and the region as a whole is one of the major natural gas reserves of North America. Alberta alone provided 86 per cent of the industry's production in 1974. The inset to Map 23 shows the detailed distribution of these fields, and serves to correct the general impression that hydrocarbons are continuously present, and worked, over very large areas. In fact their occurence is strictly localised to scattered groups of pools, most of which supply either oil or gas, but rarely both.

Remoteness from markets was a major problem for the early prairie oil industry. Local demand was limited, although there is now substantial refining capacity and the region has attracted industry on a considerable scale. Pipeline connection with the urban-industrial complex of eastern Canada was clearly necessary. The first pipeline was built in 1950 via Winnipeg to the American port of Superior, Wisconsin. The oil was then carried by tankers to refineries at Sarnia, Ontario. The pipeline was later extended to western Toronto via Sarnia. A products pipeline linked the Sarnia and the Lake Ontario refineries with Montreal, though most of the Quebec market is supplied by Venezuelan and Middle Eastern imports that enter through Portland, Maine, for Montreal is of little use as an oil port because of winter freezing of the St Lawrence. Both Vancouver

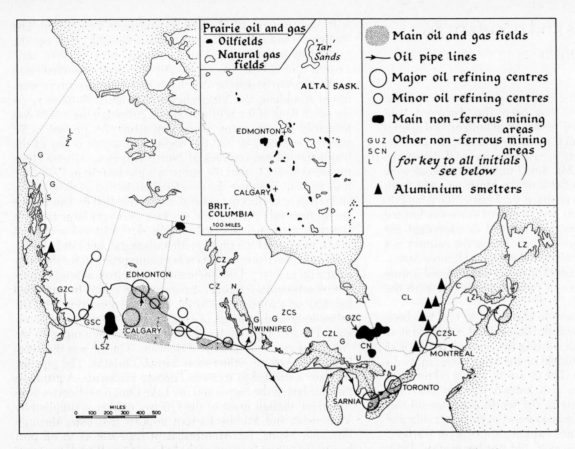

Prairie oil and gas
● Oilfields
○ Natural gas fields

'Tar' Sands

ALTA. SASK.

EDMONTON

CALGARY

BRIT. COLUMBIA

100 MILES

Main oil and gas fields

→ Oil pipe lines

◯ Major oil refining centres

○ Minor oil refining centres

■ Main non-ferrous mining areas

GUZ
SCN
L Other non-ferrous mining areas

(for key to all initials see below)

▲ Aluminium smelters

L S Z

G

G G S

G

U

G

GZC

GSC

EDMONTON

CALGARY

LSZ

U

CZ

CZ N

G G ZCS

WINNIPEG

CZL

G

CN

U

G

SARNIA

TORONTO

U

LZ

CL

C

Z

CZSL

MONTREAL

MILES
0 100 200 300 400 500

23 » Hydrocarbons and non-ferrous metals in Canada. *The detailed distribution of prairie oil and gasfields is shown in the inset.* G = Gold, U = Uranium ores, Z = Zinc, S = Silver, C = Copper, N = Nickel, L = Lead

and the Pacific North-West are supplied with prairie oil by a transmontane pipeline (cf. Map 22).

Recent co-operation with the United States authorities over the trans-shipment of Alaska gas through the Canadian north-west may make possible the opening of the gasfields of the Mackenzie Delta region on the Arctic coast. This only further emphasises, however, the abundance of western supplies in contrast to the situation in Ontario, Quebec and the Maritime Provinces. This east-west division may well become crucial in any future renegotiation of the Canadian constitution, for federal attempts to regulate western supplies to eastern advantage have already caused much animosity, complicating the western provinces' antagonism towards Quebec.

Mining has provided a major stimulus to the development of much of the Canadian Shield and the Rocky Mountains. The pre-cambrian Shield yields a great variety of metals, and the Rockies have been famous for their gold deposits.

North America's largest goldfields straddle the Ontario-Quebec boundary, at Porcupine, Larder and Kirkland Lakes. This region also possesses major resources of cobalt, zinc and silver. Of great importance are the silver, platinum and copper ores of Sudbury, Ontario, long the supplier of 90 per cent of the western world's nickel, though Thompson, Manitoba has now become a major rival source. During the 1960s major new communities were developed in north-eastern Ontario and western Quebec, but the most significant northern expansion was probably that of Pine Point on the southern shores of the Great Slave Lake where once inaccessible deposits of lead and zinc ores were opened up. South-eastern British Columbia is richly mineralised, producing lead, zinc and silver from ore bodies that are extensions of those in Idaho. Many northern settlements are remote and isolated, such as the radium-uranium deposits on the shores of Lake Athabasca. These Uranium City beds have now been surpassed by large-scale operations in the Elliot Lake region on the north shores of Lake Huron.

Given the physical limitations to further agricultural expansion these mining settlements are a major factor in the Canadian settlement of otherwise empty lands. If workings are short-lived then the problems of providing a suitable infrastructure are considerable. Such considerations are, however, overcome in the case of military installations, with strategic necessity overriding economic criteria.

24 Hydro-electric power and forest resources in eastern Canada

Eastern Canada has traditionally been the major focus for industrial development. Industries are concentrated in a linear belt from Lake Erie to the lower reaches of the St Lawrence, with specialised extensions northwards in the valleys of the Shield. The long traditions of settlement and intensive agriculture for both English and French-speaking communities in southern Ontario and in Quebec, the importance of the Great Lakes-St Lawrence route linking the interior with the Atlantic, and proximity to the United States economy have promoted industrial growth in this zone. But two distinctive advantages have shaped the industrial structure of eastern Canada: availability of cheap hydro-electric power, and access to the forest resources of the southern edge of the Shield. Cheap power and plentiful supplies of softwood have together created Canada's leading manufacturing industry, the production of wood pulp and paper, much for export to the USA. Low-cost, abundant power supply has also attracted important non-ferrous metal refining, whether from local or imported ores. In general, the development of hydro-electric potential has been almost as important to Canada as exploitation of coal was to nineteenth-century Britain.

Hydro-electric projects involve high capital costs and are now increasingly restricted to sites far from southern markets. Fortunately, however, once-remote and inaccessible sites are increasingly feasible due to improvements in transmission technology. The early developments were on a chain of easily accessible rivers descending the Shield escarpments overlooking the St Lawrence; the Ottawa-Gatineau system, the St Maurice and the Saguenay. The entire Great Lakes-St Lawrence drainage system is of post-glacial origin and there are frequent breaks in the river profile at which power can be generated. One of these, the falls of the Niagara River, is not only the site of the largest single cluster of hydro-electric plants but also one of North America's greatest tourist attractions. Further east the St Lawrence has been developed for power in the International Rapids section of the Seaway, at Beauharnois, and at the Lachine Rapids upstream from Montreal. Once-remote sites are now being exploited, as at the Rivers Bersimis, Manicougan and Outardes 200 miles below Quebec, where by the mid-1970s almost 5,000 megawatts of capacity had been installed. In Ontario the Abitipi plants supply the Sudbury smelters. The huge Shefferville iron-ore workings on the Newfoundland-Quebec boundary are now complemented by the Churchill Falls generating plant, the world's largest with over 5,000 megawatts capacity. Quebec's indigenous supplies already provide 40 per cent of Canadian capacity, with plans to double this with the development of a 12,000-megawatt system to the east of the James Bay. Objections from environmentalists and native peoples have been raised but development is progressing along the Fort George-La Grande and Eastmain River basins.

Demand for power has grown so rapidly that there has been considerable expansion of thermal power stations outside Quebec, although these market-based sites are subject to environmentalist objections; and since the early 1960s nuclear

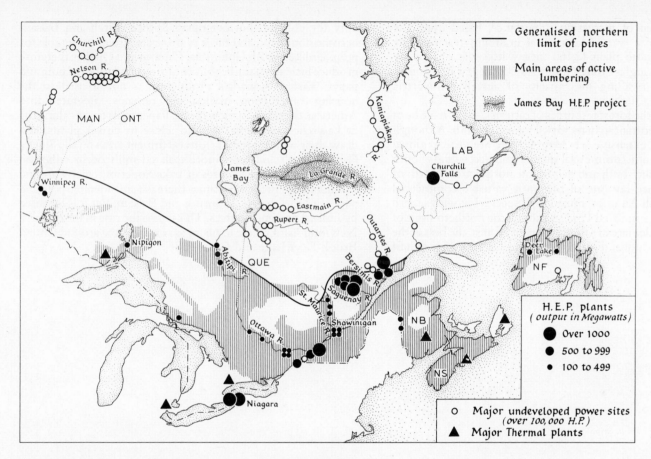

Churchill R.

Nelson R.

MAN   ONT

Winnipeg R.

Nipigon

Abitibi R.

QUE

Ottawa R.

St. Maurice R.

Shawinigan

Niagara

James Bay

La Grande R.

Eastmain R.

Rupert R.

Saguenay R.

Bersimis R.

Outardes R.

Kaniapiskau R.

LAB

Churchill Falls

NB

NS

Deer Lake

NF

	Generalised northern limit of pines
	Main areas of active lumbering
	James Bay H.E.P. project

H.E.P. plants
(output in Megawatts)

● Over 1000

● 500 to 999

• 100 to 499

○ Major undeveloped power sites
  (over 100,000 H.P.)

▲ Major Thermal plants

24 » Hydro-electric power and forest resources in eastern Canada

power has been of increasing importance, based upon the CANDU (heavy water and natural uranium) reactor. The Pickering, Ontario plant (2,160 megawatts) was on line by 1973 and the Douglas Point, Ontario (3,200 megawatts) due by 1978, thereby rivalling the capacity of new hydro-electric installations in Quebec.

Historically the forest resources of eastern Canada have been even more important than its varied mineral wealth. Although forest cover is extensive (cf. Map 4) there are great regional variations in both commercial quality and accessibility: both are highest in the south and deteriorate northwards. North of the St Lawrence lay one of the most valuable commercial forests in North America, mixed in its species but with superb stands of White and Red Pine. Although the northern limit of pines roughly demarcates this first quality forest, the best of the timber has now gone, replaced by poorer secondary growth fit only for pulping. Further north Spruce, Birch and Balsam become dominant, and most of these are also only suitable for pulp. Unlike British Columbia, Ontario and Quebec therefore produce little sawn timber but enormous quantities of pulp and paper. Eastern Canada's production is not so tied to the housing-construction market but remains integrated into American demands for newsprint. Paper mills cluster along the St Lawrence and Lake Ontario, close to power plants, and draw their wood supplies from catchment areas on the Shield. Further north and west more isolated mills occur either on railways or along the shores of Lake Superior, chiefly around Thunder Bay. In the Maritimes there is a considerable pulp and paper industry based on Spruce and Balsam, but it is localised by limited power resources. This is also the case in the island of Newfoundland where industry is concentrated around Corner Brook-Deer Lake and Great Falls.

25 The Tennessee Valley Authority

Established in 1933, the Tennessee Valley Authority (TVA) was a unique example of federal, state and local government co-operation for regional resource development. It was charged with the duty of planning the proper use, conservation and development of the natural resources of the Tennessee River basin, and by so doing to contribute to the social and economic welfare of the nation. It has successfully resisted efforts by private interests to erode the scope of its activities, but despite several attempts to create similar regional agencies the experiment has not, as yet, been successfully repeated elsewhere in the United States.

In 1933 the once fertile lands of the Tennessee valley were exhausted by decades of over-cultivation; indiscriminate felling of timber and unscientific farming techniques had left the slopes eroded and barren. The heavy rainfall of the region had swept away much of the valley's topsoil, and the river had become choked, difficult for navigation and subject to flooding. At this time of economic depression, incomes in the valley were less than half the national average. The TVA, through co-operation rather than federal imposition, was given the task of rehabilitating a region larger than New England.

Due to a long tradition of government-sponsored 'internal improvements' and conservation projects, the principles behind many of the component parts of the TVA programme were not new. But now, for the first time, they were co-ordinated in a comprehensive regional plan; each part of the Authority's multifarious activities interlocked with the rest. Dams that were built to control the rivers and prevent flooding also contained hydro-electric generating facilities. Reafforestation not only checked run-off and stopped erosion, but also helped to restore the ecological balance and enrich the soil. Contour ploughing and the encouragement of pastoral as well as arable farming also played their part. Cheap TVA power was used to produce cheap fertilisers; electricity not only brought the amenity of electric light to the region but encouraged farm mechanisation. Low-cost power and improved navigation on the river attracted industry into the valley.

The immediate problem was to control the Tennessee, the fifth longest river in the United States. Nine dams were built on the main stream and seventeen on tributaries. Another major dam was constructed on the Cumberland; six other dams in the region, owned by the Aluminum Company of America, were integrated into the system. The dams created storage reservoirs, the level of which could be regulated according to the flow of the rivers, and they have proved extremely effective in controlling floods. It is estimated that the city of Chattanooga alone was saved $100,000,000 in flood damage in a single month in the spring of 1963. The vast reservoir created by the Kentucky Dam helps to prevent flooding in the lower Ohio and Mississippi valleys; the 'Land Between the Lakes' is being developed as a vast recreation area.

Water control has made the Tennessee River navigable for inland barges and river tows with a 9-foot draught for about 650 miles upstream to Knoxville. Freight traffic on the river increased eight-fold in the first thirty years to a total of 2,500

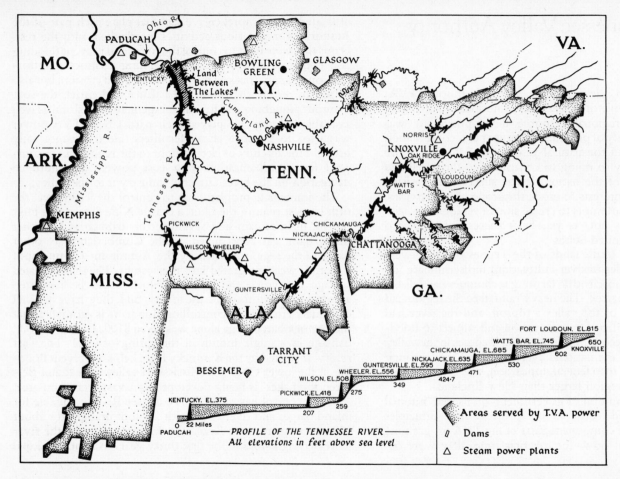

MO.

PADUCAH

Ohio R.

KENTUCKY

"Land Between The Lakes"

BOWLING GREEN

GLASGOW

VA.

KY.

Cumberland R.

NASHVILLE

NORRIS

KNOXVILLE
OAK RIDGE

FT. LOUDOUN

N. C.

ARK.

Mississippi R.

Tennessee R.

TENN.

WATTS BAR

MEMPHIS

PICKWICK

CHICKAMAUGA

NICKAJACK

CHATTANOOGA

WILSON WHEELER

MISS.

GUNTERSVILLE

ALA.

GA.

TARRANT CITY

BESSEMER

FORT LOUDOUN. EL.815

WATTS BAR. EL.745   650

CHICKAMAUGA. EL.685   KNOXVILLE

NICKAJACK.EL.635   602

GUNTERSVILLE. EL.595   530

WHEELER.EL.556   471

WILSON. EL.508   424·7

PICKWICK.EL.418   349

KENTUCKY. EL.375   275

259

207

0   22 Miles

PADUCAH

PROFILE OF THE TENNESSEE RIVER
All elevations in feet above sea level

Areas served by T.V.A. power

Dams

Steam power plants

million ton-miles a year by 1965, approximately 3 per cent of the total traffic of the vast Mississippi-Missouri-Ohio inland waterway system. A subsidiary function of the dams, which has become of major importance for the region, is the generation of electricity. The TVA not only produced power but also erected transmission lines for low-cost distribution; this provided a yardstick for reducing the high cost of privately generated electricity. Public non-profit utility systems were given priority supply. By 1942 the TVA alone was producing four times as much power as the entire region had consumed in the mid-1930s; by 1945 the Authority was supplying an area of over 80,000 square miles. Rural electrification had arrived on a large scale, facilitating industrial development and giving the rural population access to modern labour-saving devices. During the Second World War it became clear that demand, stimulated also by the needs of defence establishments such as Oak Ridge, was exceeding the capacity of the hydro-electric facilities and the TVA began to build steam plants. Demand has continued to rise since the war and there has been heavy investment in atomic energy plants. Six million people now get TVA power and the Authority operates over 20 million kilowatts of electric generating capacity.

The decision to create the TVA in 1933 was political. In an era of economic depression it was a pragmatic example of 'pump priming' by the federal government to initiate regional development. Debate however has raged as to whether a legitimate concern with promoting interstate commerce along the Tennessee River could be expanded to include power generation, soil conservation and job creation. It was initially evident that the federal concern with a stable, reliable water flow would necessarily involve rectification of social and environmental conditions that were partly responsible for making the river unnavigable, particularly the antiquated farming techniques in the valley. As its comprehensive programmes developed the TVA was characterised as both the farmer's friend and a ruthless, undemocratic foretaste of state socialism. Its constitutionality was, however, sustained by the Supreme Court and attempts to sell off the component parts of the Authority have been resisted, increasingly from within the region. Such regional development has come to be seen as a legitimate concern of the federal government where private enterprise and state governments are unwilling or unable to provide the necessary infrastructure for economic growth. But further attempts to promote regional development elsewhere, such as in Appalachia as a whole, have failed to generate comparable success, perhaps because they lack the visible focus that the river provides for the TVA.

26 The iron and steel industry of North America

The present distribution of the North American iron and steel industry is partly the result of industrial inertia: some centres remain active although the original reasons for their development have disappeared. In the early nineteenth century the first major concentrations of iron smelting developed in the valleys of eastern Pennsylvania when anthracite from the rich local coalfield (cf. Map 20) replaced charcoal as blast-furnace fuel. Local iron-ore resources, although now of limited significance, were ample by the standards of the day; the region was also located centrally in relation to the eastern seaboard market. This oldest of America's metallurgical districts is still a leading steel producer, although both its fuel and ore supplies now come from distant sources: coking coal is supplied from West Virginia, and most of its iron ore from Labrador, Venezuela and Liberia.

By the 1840s the iron industry had crossed the Appalachians, and western Pennsylvania was beginning to rival the older region to the east. At first widely scattered in the valleys around Pittsburgh, the industry still used charcoal at a time when this fuel had been supplanted elsewhere; the first coke-fired furnace was not built in Pittsburgh until 1859. Benefiting from local coking coal the city and its immediate hinterland then, until about 1900, attracted most of the new investment in steel making and in 1894 the region was producing 43 per cent of the total national output. However, new sites on the shores of Lakes Erie and Michigan were being exploited that were better placed for tapping both new sources of raw materials and the developing interior market. Since 1911, although Pittsburgh mills have extensively been rebuilt, the city recently connected to the interstate freeway system, and the downtown area redeveloped, no completely new plant has been located there, and the region has continued to lose productive capacity. Today, although Pittsburgh is no less involved in steel making than in its prime, its contribution is rather through administration and control. The city of Andrew Carnegie is still the headquarters of the United States Steel Corporation.

During the period of expansion Pittsburgh's iron ore came from the high-quality haematites of the Lake Superior region, particularly the Mesabi and Marquette 'ore ranges'. The new steel mills at Buffalo, Cleveland and Detroit could more easily and cheaply 'import' their ore supplies and, at the same time, through a complex schedule of freight rates, secure Pittsburgh coking coal cheaply by rail as 'back-loaded' cargo. Youngstown developed midway between Pittsburgh and the Erie shore, but the greatest development took place around the southern tip of Lake Michigan. Iron and steelmaking in Chicago date from the 1880s, but massive expansion in the area began in 1906 with the opening of the Gary works across the Indiana line. The region's favourable location for both materials and markets, Chicago's role as a rail centre and its general industrial vitality confirmed the hegemony of this industrial complex. It has become the major steel-producing area in North America.

The importance of coastal locations, in providing access to raw materials and cutting freight charges for finished products, also stimulated development on the Atlantic seaboard. The rebuilt Sparrows Point near Baltimore is now the world's largest single steelworks, and the Morrisville works on the Delaware enjoys comparable advantage. These sites indicate the importance for both Bethlehem Steel and United States Steel of continued access to high-grade ore supplies despite the exhaustion of domestic resources and the increased use of low-grade taconite deposits.

Inland steel plants on the Great Lakes have been fortunate in securing access to Canadian high-grade ores. The St Lawrence Seaway has made the Labrador ores as accessible as the traditional Lake Superior ones without the need for massive relocation of plants. Partly to ameliorate the increasingly critical loss of jobs in the Lake Superior fields, far from alternative sources of employment, the almost unlimited reserves of low-grade taconite and jaspilite are now being developed. 'Beneficiation' produces high-grade pellets easy to handle, less liable to freezing once stockpiled, requiring less smelting fuel and so allowing greater furnace productivity. Such domestic supplies are secure from foreign expropriation and reduce the industries' impact upon the foreign-trade deficit.

Elsewhere steel plants serve only localised, regional markets, and together provide only 10 per cent of the United States' capacity. In the southern Appalachians locally available coal and iron ore around Birmingham provided the base for Alabama's steel industry. The initial advantage of its cheap local resources was undermined by the commercial burden of the 'Pittsburgh Plus' system whereby all steel was priced as if it had been produced in and shipped from Pittsburgh. Though declared illegal in 1924 this policy successfully discouraged peripheral plants in favour of the industry's major investments in western Pennsylvania. Recently Alabama's share of the growing southern market has been undercut by ores imported via Mobile, and by the Houston and Lone Star plants in Texas.

In the West steel making reflects the interplay of three factors: strategic necessity to supply war industries in the 1940s; the growing market for steel in the post-war years, particularly in California's massive urban expansion; and the availability of localised coking coal and ores at scattered sites throughout the West. Increasingly, though, such plants as Fontana, outside Los Angeles, Geneva, south of Salt Lake City, and Pueblo south of Denver utilise scrap. The Duluth plant serving the Lake Superior ranges was built as a response to political pressures within Minnesota but remains remote from the main markets. Access to recently developed western coal may improve its competitiveness. Most demand, however, is generated in the Atlantic and Great Lakes manufacturing areas, which effectively limits steel making elsewhere.

The Canadian industry has four main centres. The steelworks at Sydney, on Cape Breton Island, depends upon local coal and Newfoundland ore. At Bécancour, Labrador ores supply Quebec's steel plant. Sault Ste Marie and Hamilton, Ontario, have access to cheap lake transport from the Lake Superior ranges with coal from Appalachia. The favoured location of Hamilton in relation to the Windsor-Toronto-Montreal axis, the industrial heartland of Canada, make Hamilton by far the most important Canadian producer. Since the opening of the St Lawrence Seaway in 1959 Canadian mills, like the lakeshore mills of the United States, have been able to obtain iron ore at competitive rates from the huge deposits of

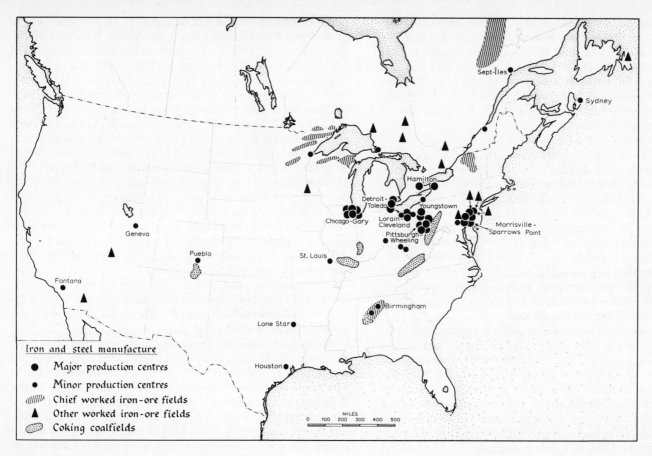

Sept-Îles

Sydney

Hamilton

Detroit-
Toledo

Chicago-Gary

Youngstown

Lorain
Cleveland

Pittsburgh-
Wheeling

Morrisville-
Sparrows Point

Geneva

Pueblo

St. Louis

Fontana

Birmingham

Lone Star

Houston

Iron and steel manufacture
- ● Major production centres
- • Minor production centres
- ||||| Chief worked iron-ore fields
- ▲ Other worked iron-ore fields
- ⬭ Coking coalfields

MILES
0 100 200 300 400 500

26 » The iron and steel industry of North America

Quebec and Labrador. Construction of concentrator and pellet plants at Sept Îles on the St Lawrence have greatly enhanced both Quebec's and Canada's effective capacity to supply North American industry, but the world recession has necessitated massive stockpiling. Total steel production in the United States doubled between 1940 and 1966 to 134 million tonnes. This fell with the 1970 recession to 119 million tonnes but rose by 1974 back to 132 million tonnes. Canadian production enjoyed greater rates of growth but still only reached 14 million tonnes by 1974.

27 The regional distribution of manufacturing in the USA

The series of Maps 27 to 29, showing the general distribution of manufacturing in the United States, uses a progressively finer analysis from region to state to city; Map 30 indicates the pattern of regional change since 1945. Manufacturing activity can be measured in several different ways related to the general factors of production, labour, capital and raw materials. Three comparative measures are illustrated on Maps 27a and 27b: number of production workers, total payroll of manufacturing workers, and 'value added by manufacturing' (A – C); these are shown as regional shares of national totals.

The simplest and most direct measure is the number of production workers, but the productivity of labour varies regionally and between industries so that employment is not, by itself, an adequate yardstick. Labour is merely one of several 'inputs' into the industrial process, and an 'output' measure is also necessary: the best is 'value added by manufacturing', that is, the net value of total manufactured products. Total manufacturing payroll is also indicated, for this not only reflects the size of the labour 'input' but also the value of 'output' expressed in industrial wages. A useful compromise measure, it forms the basis for the analysis of manufacturing by states on Map 28.

Maps 27a and 27b reveal sharp regional contrasts persisting into the 1970s. Whichever index is used, New England contains less than 8 per cent of the nation's manufacturing, only half its relative share at the end of the nineteenth century. The Middle Atlantic region contains about 20 per cent of total manufacturing workers, compared with 24 per cent in 1963 and 34 per cent in 1899. Its higher share of total manufacturing payroll, together with its lower share of 'value added', reflects the high proportion of technical and white-collar workers, for much of the research activities and the administration of American industry is centred here. The East North Central region, the industrial Midwest, is the leading manufacturing area. With 26 per cent of national manufacturing employment, only a slight increase of 3 per cent since 1899, midwestern industry accounts for almost 30 per cent of manufacturing payroll and 'value added', indicating that its importance is greater than its share of employment suggests, a feature that has remained stable over the last decade. In the South Atlantic region the reverse remains true: although containing just over 14 per cent of the nation's manufacturing workers, it accounts for less than 12 per cent of the total payroll, a situation that has been essentially static despite the talk of southern expansion. The East South Central region, and also the West South Central, despite the industrial development within Texas, each still contributes only about 6 per cent of total manufacturing payroll. Like the West North Central region with 6 per cent, they have only maintained their relative position since 1899. The share of the Mountain West is still trivial, but the states of the West Coast have increased their share of manufacturing employment from 3 per cent to about 10 per cent; by 'value added' and total manufacturing payroll they now claim almost 12 per cent of the national total of manufacturing.

It is clear that the Manufacturing Belt, stretching from Mas-

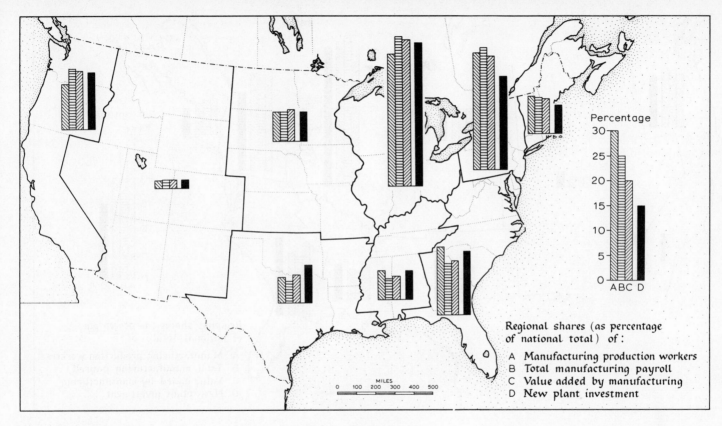

Percentage

30
25
20
15
10
5
0
A B C D

Regional shares (as percentage of national total) of:

A Manufacturing production workers
B Total manufacturing payroll
C Value added by manufacturing
D New plant investment

MILES
0   100 200 300 400 500

27a » The regional distribution of manufacturing in the USA, 1963 figures

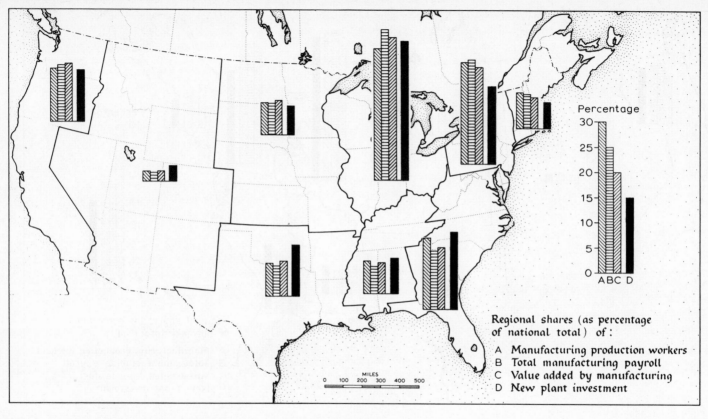

Percentage

Regional shares (as percentage of national total) of:

A Manufacturing production workers
B Total manufacturing payroll
C Value added by manufacturing
D New plant investment

MILES
0 100 200 300 400 500

27b » The regional distribution of manufacuting in the USA, 1973 figures

sachusetts to Illinois, still dominates the industrial scene with 53 per cent of all production workers, although this is a drop of 5 per cent over ten years. Except for growth in the West, particularly in California, there has been little radical decentralisation of industry on a regional scale. Regional redistribution is discussed in relation to Map 30, but one measure of change, new plant investment, is included on the maps here (D). Relating each to a single year, these figures must be treated with great caution; nevertheless, together they indicate an underlying reality. The regional distribution of new plant investment provides a useful, albeit approximate, indication of current trends in industrial growth.

The picture, however, is confused by the nature and extent of the officially designated census regions. These cut across integrated areas of economic development, often combining very dissimilar areas, for example Maryland's great commercial and industrial development is grouped with its traditional southern neighbours rather than with the Middle Atlantic region of which its economy is now an integral part.

28 The distribution of manufacturing in the USA by state

Contrasts in the distribution of manufacturing industry, at the state level, are summarised in two ways: the percentage share of each state in the total national manufacturing payroll is the direct measure of its importance in the industrial economy of the nation; the *per capita* size of the manufacturing payroll generated in each state is a complementary measure of the intensity of development. As on Maps 27a and 27b, regional patterns emerge.

The region of most intensive manufacturing reaches from southern New England into the eastern Midwest between the Ohio and the Mississippi Rivers: this is the 'manufacturing belt' redefined. Six of the twelve states still contribute at least 5 per cent of the total manufacturing payroll, though New York's dominant 11 per cent fell to 9 per cent over the decade, indicative of a shift of focus within the Manufacturing Belt into the Midwest. Around the margins of the industrial North-East lies a band of states where manufacturing is not so developed, each contributing between 1 per cent and 2 per cent of the national manufacturing payroll. West Virginia's decline emphasises its continuing poverty despite great mineral wealth (cf. Map 20). The south-eastern states have gained somewhat in employment as the North-East has declined, but remain far behind in absolute terms. However, on a *per capita* basis North Carolina, with its textiles and research based development, has joined the industrial heartland. Texan development is noticeable over the decade, but is less impressive in relation to its vast

area, and is strongly localised in its southern and eastern parts; Texas's more significant role remains that of a primary producer in the US economy (cf. Maps 21 to 22). To the north the tier of states from Minnesota to Kansas contains only a few significant manufacturing cities set within a predominantly rural economy.

Linking east and west a bridge of states persists, reaching West from Kansas via Colorado, Utah and Arizona to the Pacific coast. In Colorado and Utah manufacturing is based upon metallurgical industries, but aerospace and electronic interests expanded during the period of the Cold War, reflecting partly their strategic location, partly easy access to suitable testing grounds. California has enjoyed similar conditions, with expansion successively promoted by the oil, film and aircraft industries. A highly diversified economy developed, particularly in the southern part of the state, to serve its growing population. Otherwise the Pacific states are still highly dependent upon farm and forest products, though the location of the Boeing Aircraft Corporation at Seattle has maintained Washington's contribution to the national manufacturing economy.

In contrasting the situations in 1963 and 1973 the impact of continued inflation must be borne in mind. Nevertheless the overall picture remains that of dominance by the manufacturing belt. This dominance, however, is focussed on the more traditional sectors of manufacturing that are no longer the leading growth areas. New industries increasingly find the southern states, with their less energy-consuming climates, and a less unionised labour force, attractive for development. Increasingly regional competition may come to be rivalry between the 'sunbelt' and the 'snowbelt'.

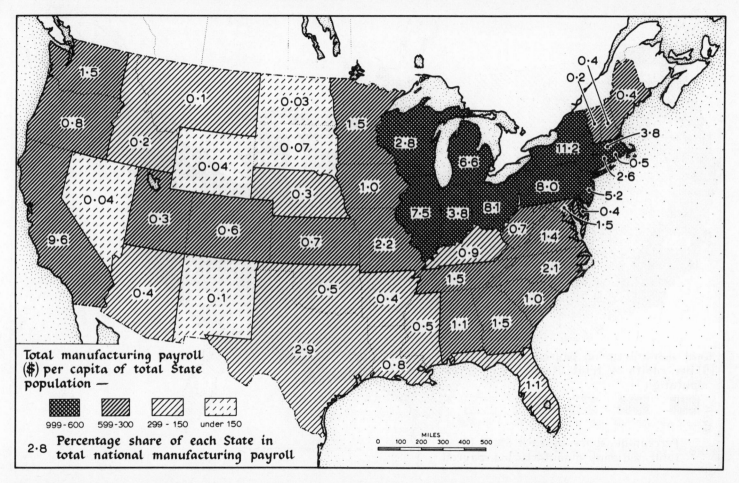

Total manufacturing payroll ($) per capita of total State population —

999-600 | 599-300 | 299-150 | under 150

2.8 Percentage share of each State in total national manufacturing payroll

MILES
0 100 200 300 400 500

28a » The distribution of manufacturing in the USA by state, 1963 figures

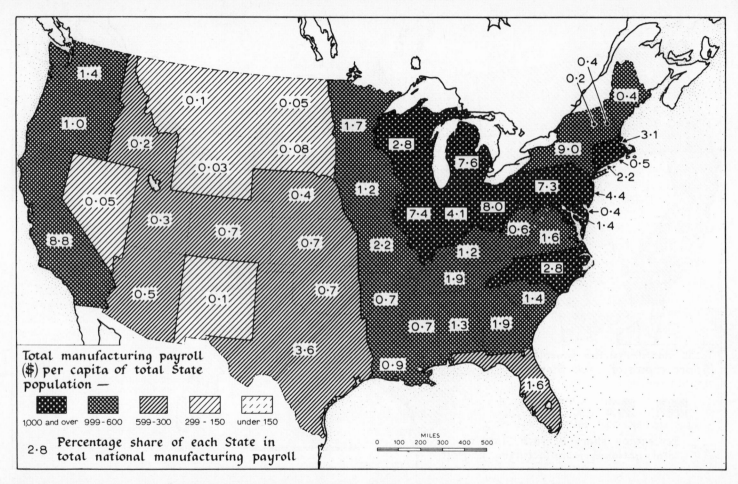

28b ≫ The distribution of manufacturing in the USA by state, 1973 figures

Total manufacturing payroll ($) per capita of total State population —

1,000 and over   999 - 600   599 - 300   299 - 150   under 150

2·8   Percentage share of each State in total national manufacturing payroll

MILES
0   100   200   300   400   500

29 The major manufacturing cities of North America

It is convenient and illuminating to describe the distribution of manufacturing in terms of state and regional patterns, but industry is concentrated within and around cities, especially the larger urban complexes. Measured in terms of 'value added' about 94 per cent of United States manufacturing was, in 1972, concentrated in the Standard Metropolitan Statistical Areas with a population of 200,000 or more. Although there has been a long-term shift of manufacturing from the central city to the periphery, and some 'drift' of industry from the metropolitan areas to smaller towns, the great cities retain their hold. Thus the pair of maps presented here, showing cities with more than 40,000 industrial workers, portrays the urban distribution of the bulk of American manufacturing. Similarly defined Candian cities are also shown.

The Manufacturing Belt is clearly bi-nodal, with two great clusters of cities. Along the Atlantic seaboard, based on New York, stretches that great corridor of urban development from Boston to Washington, DC often called 'Megalopolis' and containing over forty million people. Its relative significance is declining. Some industries, such as New England textiles, are contracting; other sectors, for example the research-based industries of Massachusetts, have grown. Overall this historic core of America's industrialisation consistently has secured the smallest regional share of total industrial growth in recent years. The rival cluster of cities sprawls along the shores of the Great Lakes. Chicago and Detroit-Cleveland are the centres of industrial regions containing a number of substantial manufacturing towns. Although their economies are based upon iron and steel (cf. Map 26), the Lakeshore cities have a greater share of growth industries than their eastern competitors; their relative position is now much stronger than it was sixty years ago. With the suburbanisation of much modern industry the plight of inner-city areas, however, has become acute as unemployment rises.

Between these two dominant areas on the Atlantic seaboard and the Great Lakes lies a region of less intensive industrial development. Despite its coalfield location and historic role this region has no industrial city of the first order except Pittsburgh, which continues to link the east coast with the interior, though under severe competition, as in the past, from the corridor of manufacturing centres along the Hudson-Mohawk routeway, via Rochester and Buffalo to Lake Erie.

Within narrower limits the Canadian manufacturing belt is also bi-nodal. Its western concentration, running from Toronto to Windsor, across the border from Detroit, is almost entirely distinct from the great port of Montreal, though as comparison between the maps indicates Toronto has overtaken its long-time rival.

The dominance of the Manufacturing Belt in both Canada and the United States is such that the rest of both maps is relatively empty. The South-East continues to lack a single manufacturing city of great size, though Greenville has emerged on the Piedmont. However, Dallas, Texas,has grown to equal all but the giants Chicago and New York, and St Louis, Missouri, is still capitalising upon its position as 'Gate-

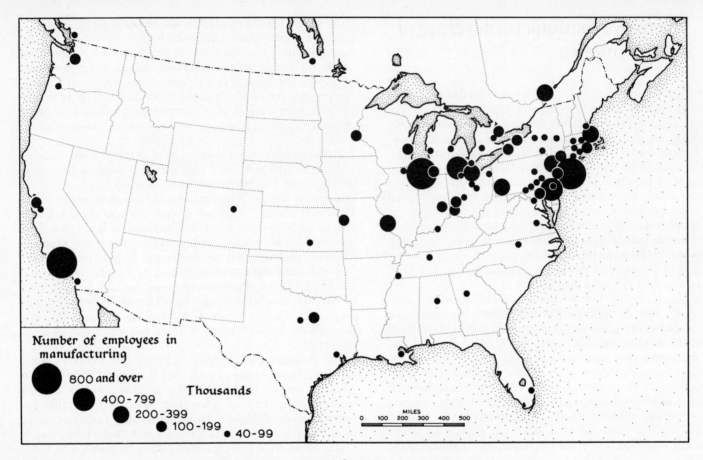

29a » The major manufactuing cities of North America, 1962 figures

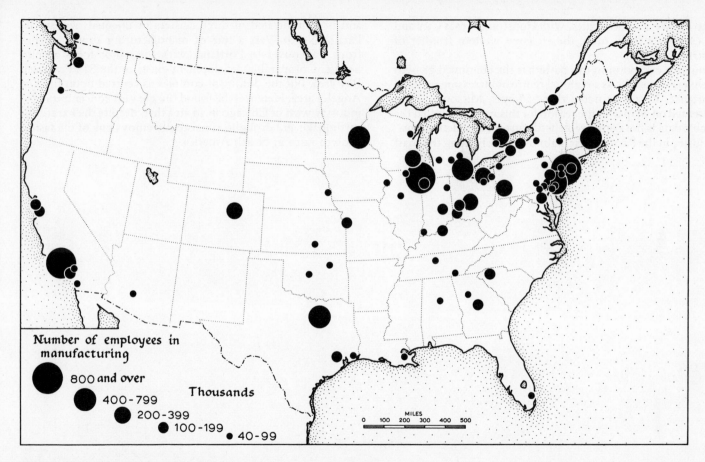

29b » The major manufacturing cities of North America, 1972 figures

way to the West'. These cities, with Houston, Kansas City and Minneapolis-St Paul, mark the effective western frontier of industrial America.

A notable exception to this pattern is the continued growth of Denver, Colorado, as a regional centre of increasing national importance. It will be noted that St Louis, Missouri, is not represented on Map 29b; the reason for this omission is that the available data is not comparable with current area definitions.

Industry in the Pacific West is almost entirely along the coast and is concentrated in three clusters of unequal size. In the Pacific North-West a line of manufacturing towns reaches from Vancouver to Portland, with the major focus around Seattle. Comparable development exists in the San Francisco Bay area, but the dominant complex is centred upon the Los Angeles area. Here is to be found the greatest concentration of industry west of Chicago in an area that, despite the hazards of earthquake and drought, consistently enjoys one of the fastest growth rates in North America.

30 Regional change in the distribution of manufacturing in the USA

It is inherently more difficult to trace change and evolution in the industrial economy than to describe that economy at particular points in time. Map 30 shows, through the regional distribution of new manufacturing employment between 1947 and 1973, where the tremendous industrial growth of the USA has been located. Each region is credited with its percentage share of the total national increase; decreases are omitted, partly in the interests of clarity but also to avoid misleading conclusions. Neither a relative nor an absolute fall in employment is necessarily a sign of industrial weakness: it may reflect massive investment in new technology and therefore an improvement in labour productivity.

Such problems of interpretation are best illustrated with reference to the Middle Atlantic region. During the period 1947 to 1958 the states in this region suffered a distinct decline in their share of national manufacturing employment growth, and there was only a trivial 1 per cent recovery between 1958 and 1963. No further growth was recorded between 1963 and 1973. By this measure, then, the region did not share in the expansion of the post-war years. On the other hand it claimed 22 per cent of the national increase in the value added by manufacturing for the period 1947 to 1958, and a consistent 17 per cent share for the periods 1958 to 1963 and 1963 to 1973. In spite of a stable, and in some states a diminishing, labour input, the Middle Atlantic states have raised industrial output by greater productivity from the same size of labour force as in 1947. The number of low-paid manual workers has decreased, but automation and technological progress have increased the proportion of high-paid employment. This is not a region of industrial stagnation, as the map might suggest, but of considerable progress that does not find expression in significant growth of employment. The price, though, is paid by those communities, especially in the inner cities of the largest metropolitan areas, where structural unemployment undermines the ability of minority groups to enter the economic mainstream.

Such changes of great social importance have not been restricted to the Middle Atlantic region. Growth in industrial output without employment increase was general throughout the three regions of the manufacturing belt between 1947 and 1958, for New England and the industrial Midwest were also redeploying labour, and so improving their industrial strength. Although interpreted at the time as massive industrial decentralisation, the period was rather one of rapid technological and structural change. Even the apparent stagnation did not persist in the second period: New England attracted a small but significant share in the national increase in industrial employment between 1958 and 1963, as the textile base gave way to sophisticated engineering. This was not repeated between 1963 and 1973, but in the industrial Midwest a substantial 22 per cent increase in the middle period was followed by another increase of 25 per cent. Even this fails to measure the Midwest's performance accurately, for its share of the increase in 'value added' was over 30 per cent between 1958 and 1963 and 27 per cent between 1963 and 1973.

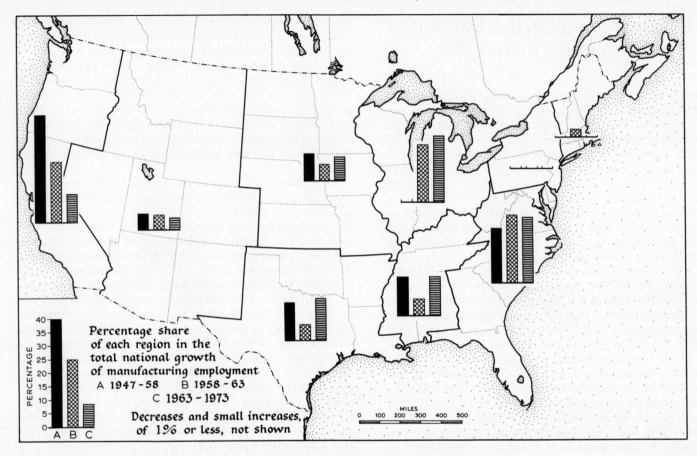

Percentage share
of each region in the
total national growth
of manufacturing employment
A 1947–58   B 1958–63
C 1963–1973
Decreases and small increases,
of 1% or less, not shown

PERCENTAGE

40
35
30
25
20
15
10
5
0

A B C

MILES
0 100 200 300 400 500

30 » Regional change in the distribution of manufacturing in the USA, 1947–73

Outside the industrial heartland all regions secured some share of employment growth throughout the whole post-1947 period. The South Atlantic and East South Central regions both gained an increasing share, and to this extent decentralisation has occurred. Expansion in the South Atlantic states rivals that in the East North Central industrial region, both with 26 per cent over the decade 1963 to 1973. Much of this part of the South, however, is an area of labour-intensive industries such as textiles, and its performance has been poorer in terms of 'value added', though developments in the 'research triangle' of North Carolina are beginning to counter this. Industrial growth in the West South Central states, mainly Texas, has regained some ground lost between 1958 and 1963, whereas the Pacific West seems to be steadily losing momentum, failing to secure as large a share as in the immediate post-war era. The dispersion of much aerospace business and the lack of major energy supplies seems to be taking its toll. The Pacific West's 14 per cent share in the national increase in 'value added' between 1958 and 1963 fell to 11 per cent over the next decade, whilst a 22 per cent share in employment growth fell to 9 per cent. There is thus substantial evidence that the great industrial expansion of the Pacific West is beginning to slow down.

31 Railroad density in the USA

American railroads played a vital role both in the development of the national economy and in determining the regional balance of power. The federal government used the railroad companies as agents for settling the West (cf. Map 10) and the age of railroad dominance of transportation extends into the twentieth century. Track mileage actually reached a peak in the 1920s but then, in the face of severe competition from road and later air transport, and also from pipelines, a number of routes became unprofitable and were closed. Between 1930 and 1972 route mileage declined from 260,000 to 218,000 miles.

Long-distance passenger services on a European or even Canadian scale are no longer available in the United States. A study by the Interstate Commerce Commission in 1968 concluded that passenger revenues over the previous fourteen years had slightly exceeded operating expenses. But the 360 companies insisted that, when all costs were taken into account, passenger services were uneconomic and offered little potential for future profitability in competition with the automobile within cities and the bus and 'plane in the inter-city market. The near monopoly of inter-city passenger movement held by the railroads in 1920 had fallen to less than 1 per cent in 1972. Severe economies had been made and the closure of stations, failure to maintain tracks, and deliberate use of old rolling-stock had discouraged custom. By 1960 many cities with over one million people, such as Cleveland, were without passenger services. Even commuter services into the cities were run down, despite the social need involved. Deterioration of facilities was such that in 1970 the federal government intervened to save the remaining skeletal passenger service. The Rail Passenger Service Act relieved the private companies of many of their passenger routes. Reorganisation was based upon improving passenger services between twenty-one pairs of cities as nodes for a future network, but most concern has focussed upon supplying the highly urbanised north-east corridor with high-speed trains, particularly between Washington and New York, to relieve the overburdened highways and air-shuttle services. Amtrak, a public corporation set up in 1971 to run a national passenger network, has tried with some success to win passengers back to the railroads, but the legacy of the years of poor track maintenance impeded the rapid development of an attractive and efficient service. Annual deficits mounted, and by 1979 plans were being discussed to eliminate over a third of Amtrak's 27,500-mile system.

Freight services have not suffered in like fashion. Despite a decline in their share of the market the volume of freight carried has continued to rise and they remain profitable. Ton mileage almost doubled between 1940 and 1972, much of this increase being in the highly profitable long-haul business. American railroads have accepted the competition from road transport and pipelines by the introduction of integrated services, such as 'piggy-back' trains to carry trucks, and long-haul unit trains for mineral traffic. By 1973 they derived 92 per cent of their revenue from freight, and retained 38 per cent of this market. The remaining rail network is being used with greater intensity and improved efficiency. To meet the needs of west-

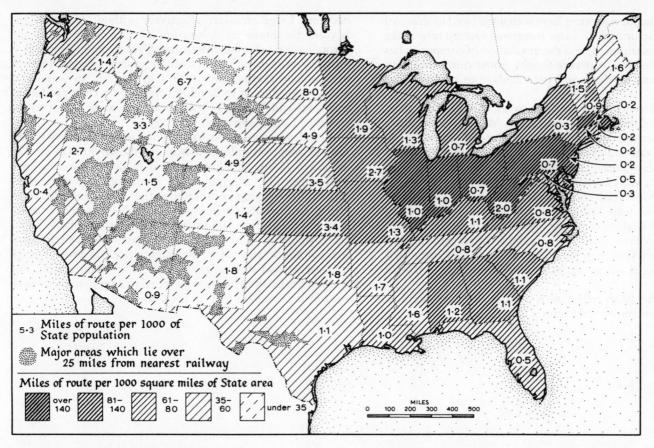

Miles of route per 1000 of State population

5·3 ● Miles of route per 1000 of
State population

∴ ● Major areas which lie over
25 miles from nearest railway

Miles of route per 1000 square miles of State area

over 140 | 81–140 | 61–80 | 35–60 | under 35

MILES
0 100 200 300 400 500

31 » Density of the railroad network in the USA. *The two measures employed show regional contrast in railroad provision, 1974 figures*

ern strip mining new services have been introduced to ship coal to the manufacturing belt. Large integrated systems now make better use of equipment, and the installation of computers has greatly speeded long-distance freight. Some companies have diversified into pipelines and road haulage to increase their profitability.

The complexity of the railroad network makes it difficult to map individual lines without confusion. Map 31 has therefore been constructed to show general intensity and regional variations in the railroad system by showing railroad mileage in relation to state area. The region with the most intensive development clearly corresponds with the manufacturing belt, and close networks still serve the Corn, Wheat and Dairy Belts and the Appalachian coalfield. Heavy traffic in bulk products flows profitably along the dense midwestern network. Parts of the South also have a high ratio of railroad mileage to area: the well-developed system in the heart of the onetime Cotton Belt reflects the need to get agricultural commodities to distant markets.

West of the 100th meridian is a more skeletal system of east-west transcontinental routes with relatively few intercon-nections. Large areas are effectively without railroads, and beyond the limits of cultivation on the Great Plains and throughout much of the Mountain West are huge segments of territory more than 25 miles from the nearest railroad. The lack of complete railroad penetration in this region was not a serious impediment to development, for the chief product of this semi-arid West was lean cattle that were driven to the railheads for shipment (cf. Map 19).

A crude measure of the market potential for rail service is the ratio of people to mileage that is also shown on Map 31. The urbanised North-East has a very high ratio generating high traffic densities, although near metropolitan centres these include loss-making commuter traffic. In the rural Midwest traffic densities are much lower, passenger services are minimal, and the traffic is almost entirely freight. The thinly populated Mountain West has never generated much traffic apart from minerals and cattle, although there has been a recent increase in coal shipments from the strip-mining areas, and most densities along these lines are related more to their transcontinental function than to local needs.

32 Canadian railways

Despite competition, Canadian railways have remained the country's most important means of transportation. Air and road transport are even more seriously disrupted by the extreme winter conditions than the railways, and the overwhelming importance in the national economy of primary agricultural and mining industries underlines the importance of the railways as bulk carriers. Rail connections with Atlantic ports are particularly important during the winter freezing of the St Lawrence.

The first railway was opened in Quebec in 1836, but by 1850 there were still only 66 miles of track in the whole of Canada. In the early 1850s, however, a railway boom began when the Grand Trunk line was opened linking Toronto and Montreal with Portland, Maine. The British North America Act of 1867 included an agreement to build rail connections between the four provinces, and the Intercolonial Railway to Halifax was opened in 1876. Similarly, one of the conditions of British Columbia's accession to the Confederation in 1871 was the construction of a transcontinental railway: this, the Canadian Pacific, was opened in 1885. Like most of the American transcontinentals, it was subsidised by a land grant amounting to over 26 million acres. With the rush of immigration into the Prairie Provinces after 1890 a network of feeder lines spread across the West and two new transcontinental systems were built. The Grand Trunk Pacific was constructed from Prince Rupert, British Columbia, to connect with the government-owned National Transcontinental Railway at Winnipeg, so providing additional through services between the Pacific and Atlantic coasts; the Canadian Northern system was pieced together from Vancouver to Montreal. Although the older CPR thrived, the later lines, because of overbuilding and the slowing of immigration due to the First World War, were in serious financial difficulties by 1917. Within six years they had been taken over by the federal government and combined into the Canadian National Railway.

The CNR is the larger of the two main systems, running over 22,000 miles of track in Canada and 2,000 in the United States; it is the only company operating in all ten provinces. In addition to rail services it controls a scheduled airline, a fleet of coastal steamers, and a number of hotels and resorts. The CPR is slightly smaller with 21,000 miles of track, but its domestic and international airline and shipping services are considerably more extensive than those of the CNR. In addition to these two giants smaller railways serve isolated mining communities on the Shield and the settlements around Hudson Bay and in the Peace River country.

Total track mileage in 1965, although small in comparison with that in the United States, was, unlike the American system, still expanding. 1,500 miles were opened between 1955 and 1965, and a further 500 miles planned. By 1975 total track mileage seemed to have stabilised at around the 60,000 level that was reached in 1972, recent expansion having been mainly in freight lines. The role of the railways as bulk carriers is confirmed: freight tonnage has increased steadily since the end of the Second World War and in 1975 was over 280 million

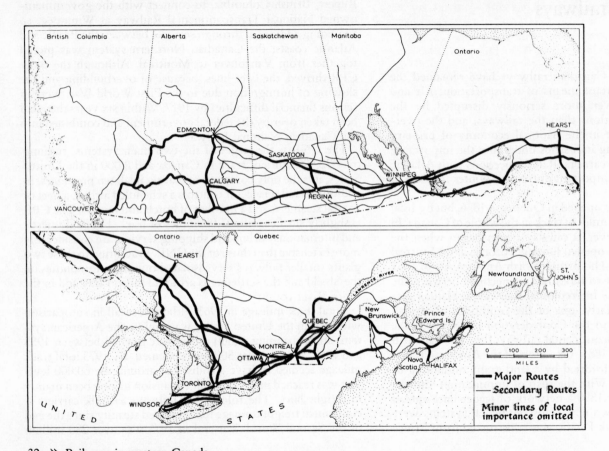

32a » Railways in western Canada
32b » Railways in eastern Canada
    Transcontinentals and major freight routes are shown

tons. Although this represented a 10 per cent decrease over the previous year, explanations are to be found in a number of rail and port strikes and in adverse economic conditions rather than declining competitiveness of the railway industry. Indeed its efficiency has been improved by containerisation and the development of bulk tankers. Passenger traffic climbed through the 1960s but peaked in 1967 and has since shown a steady decline. By 1975 it had fallen below the level of 1960, reflecting the expansion of aviation services and increased use of the motor car. In general, however, Canadian railways are run efficiently and profitably, have exploited technological developments, and are well equipped to fulfil their vital role in the national economy.

33 Interstate and superhighway system of North America

In the United States financial assistance from the federal government to the states for 'internal improvements', including road construction, dates from the early years of the Republic. The rapid development of the automobile in the early twentieth century gave a new urgency to road building; and in 1916 the Office, later the Bureau, of Public Roads began to administer an expanding and more coherent programme of federal aid. Other federal agencies, such as the National Park Service and the Bureau of Indian Affairs, made specialised contributions in particular areas. In 1944 the proposed National System of Interstate and Defense Highways provided for federal assistance of up to 50 per cent of cost on a matching basis with state contributions, but for the next ten years congress appropriated only modest funds for the development of the system. The Federal-Aid Highway Act of 1956 increased the federal contribution to 90 per cent and envisaged a network of 41,000 miles of Interstate Highways.

The stated purpose was to connect the major metropolitan centres and industrial areas by limited access, high-speed roads; links with Canada and Mexico were to be made at appropriate border crossings. A comparison of Maps 33, 29 and 37 shows the extent to which this purpose has been fulfilled. The system was designed to improve the nation's defence potential in the event of war, but has made a major contribution to the national economy: throughout its development it has significantly speeded the flow of goods and people across the country. The Interstate Highways have been financed through the Federal Highway Trust Fund, established by the Highway Revenue Act of 1956 and built up from federal tax receipts on motor vehicles, fuel and automotive products. In 1956 over $4,129 million was spent by the Fund, and by the end of 1967 over three-quarters of the network had been opened to traffic, with incalculable benefits to a country where almost ninety-six million motor vehicles of all types were registered in 1966. By the mid-1970s the major network had been connected although new projects continue to be added according to the demands of continued urban expansion. Motor vehicle registrations of all types rose to over 133 million by 1975, with over 125 million licensed drivers in a total pupulation of 213·5 million.

In Canada also the scale and size of the country has challenged the resources of communication but, although three out of four families own cars, the relatively small and concentrated population has not as yet required a dense national network of high-speed roads. Apart from the 'Roads to Resources' and 'Development Roads' programmes, the major contribution of the federal government has been made in the construction of the Trans-Canada Highway. In 1949 agreements were made with the provincial governments to build a transcontinental road along the shortest practicable route, with the Dominion government bearing almost two-thirds of the cost. With the closing of the last major gap through the Rocky Mountains in 1962 the entire 4,860 mile highway from Sydney, NS to Vancouver, BC was officially opened to traffic. As in the United States, local 'thruways' connect the main urban centres and provide rapid communications that have facilitated the growth of the trucking industry.

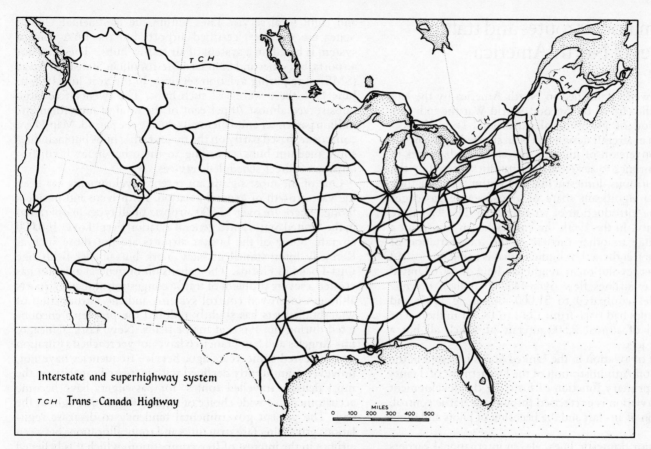

Interstate and superhighway system

TCH Trans-Canada Highway

MILES

0   100   200   300   400   500

33 » Interstate and superhighway system of the USA and southern Canada

34 The major air routes and traffic centres of North America

Aviation was well established in North America by the late 1930s, but at the end of the Second World War the industry entered a period of phenomenal expansion. Technological improvements in aircraft design had been spurred by the needs of war; the conversion of military aircraft to civilian uses in 1945 enabled airlines to seize the opportunities offered by the potentially enormous domestic market. Within a decade they had captured a significant share of long-distance passenger movement; the introduction of jet aircraft in the 1950s gave them dominance. In the 1960s the airlines began to present a serious challenge to other carriers in the transportation of certain types of freight, a development that is being intensified by the container revolution in freight handling. In 1976 United States domestic airlines flew over 145,000 million revenue passenger miles compared to 51,000 million in 1965; and revenue ton miles had risen from 1,661 to 18,801 million. The fleet consisted of almost 2,500 aircraft of which all but a hundred were jets.

Supervision of aviation in the United States is vested in the Federal Aviation Administration of the Department of Transportation. Its primary function of fostering the development and safety of aviation is excercised through air traffic control, the certification of aircraft and the licensing of pilots and other personnel.

The ten major domestic lines, eleven international carriers and eight local service lines within the continental United States use over 600 certified airports but the FAA control system is based on a system of air traffic 'hubs'. These are not airports, but cities and Standard Metropolitan Statistical Areas (SMSAs) requiring aviation services. In the year July 1975 to June 1976 there were 152 such hubs. The twenty-five large hubs served almost 70 per cent of the total of more than 207 million passenger emplanements during the period. Map 34 is a composite, based partly on the major traffic hubs but including some medium hubs according to the other index used: frequency of direct scheduled services.

One of the most significant recent developments has been the vast growth of general aviation, i.e. private and business flying. There are over 13,000 airports of all types in operation in the United States and a general aviation fleet of over 160,000 aircraft. Some of the busiest airports are not those such as Kennedy International in New York but smaller fields like Opa-Locka in Florida. The expansion of general aviation has created a severe problem of traffic congestion at many airports although improved control systems and the introduction of wide-bodied jets has slightly reduced the problems encountered during the 1960s at major fields. New York, Chicago, Los Angeles and San Francisco have not yet reached saturation as was feared some years ago. Service frequencies have not, however, significantly declined with increased capacity on the most densely travelled routes, for passengers have become accustomed to a wide choice of regular flights throughout the day. The present governmental tendency to decrease regulations governing fare structures and route allocations between airlines in the interest of free competition, which it is believed

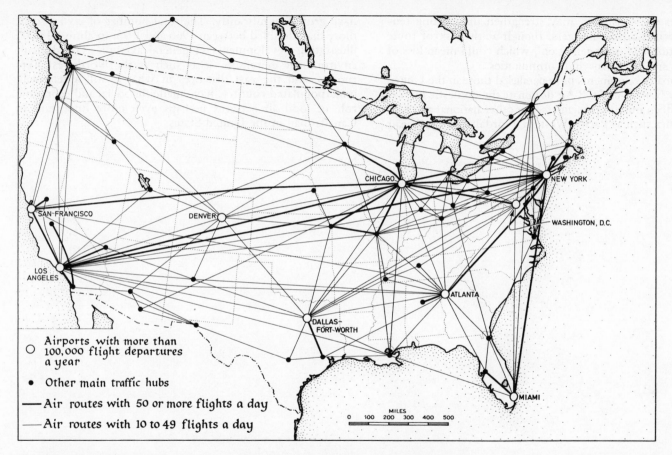

Airports with more than
○ 100,000 flight departures
a year

● Other main traffic hubs

── Air routes with 50 or more flights a day

─ Air routes with 10 to 49 flights a day

MILES
0 100 200 300 400 500

34 » The major scheduled air routes and civil airports of North America, 1976 figures

best serves the consumer, may strengthen the existing tendency towards airline mergers, though at the risk of route consolidation and 'rationalisation', which could mean loss of service to smaller towns and communities.

In Canada developments have paralleled those in the United States. Air Canada and CP Air dominate the domestic market of over fifteen million passengers, but other national and regional airlines such as Pacific Western, Nordair and Quebecair have grown significantly. The total number of civil aircraft more than doubled between 1966 and 1975, to almost 18,000 illustrating developments in general aviation. The difficult environment in remote areas such as the Northwest Territories, and the vast distances in what is still a relatively underpopulated country, have made the social and economic role of local air services perhaps even more important in Canada than in the United States.

35 The major coastal and interior ports of North America

Since 1945 foreign trade has become increasingly important to the economy of the United States. Industry and agriculture are now far more export oriented, and the value of total exports increased from $10,142 million in 1950 to $26,086 million in 1964, and then to almost $100,000 million by 1974. Imports too have risen at a rapidly increasing rate to produce an overall deficit in the balance of trade. A major item here is oil, but the total includes a number of other basic commodities once available in surplus from domestic resources. Foreign-manufactured consumer goods have also made deep inroads in the domestic market. These changes in the general economic situation are reflected in the growing importance of US ports. Canadian ports, by contrast, have traditionally played a more vital role for, until the Second World War, the Candian economy was dominated by the production of primary products that were exchanged in world markets for manufactured goods. The development of a more balanced national economy has not, however, reduced the importance of primary exports which have themselves grown to meet increasing world demand.

Map 35 shows the relative size of North American ports in terms of cargo tonnage handled, and broadly indicates the direction of this traffic. The Port of New York and those of the Delaware River and the San Francisco Bay Area dominate the map although New York has suffered a relative decline over the past decade; all show an imbalance between imports and exports and are also heavily engaged in coastwise trade. Some specialised ports handling the one-way flow of a single commodity equal in importance many of the general cargo ports. Portland, Maine, for example, is an oil port from which parts of eastern Canada as well as the eastern United States are supplied by pipeline. Norfolk and Newport News in Virginia export considerable quantities of Appalachian coal. Much of the trade of Tampa is in Florida phosphate, and New Orleans is a major exporter of cotton and other agricultural products from its extensive hinterland in the Mississippi Valley. The Texan ports of Beaumont, Port Arthur, Houston and Corpus Christi have expanded significantly in the past decade, reflecting both general economic expansion in Texas and the South-West and particular developments in petrochemicals and high-technology industries partly generated by the existence of the Houston Space Center.

The Canadian ports of Sept Îsles and Port Cartier on the St Lawrence ship Labrador iron ore and other minerals to the steel mills and industrial plants of the Atlantic seaboard and Great Lakes region. Quebec is a considerable importer of crude petroleum but the pre-eminent port of Canada remains Montreal, strong in most aspects of Canada's international and coastwise traffic, including the export of wheat. Thunder Bay, by contrast, loads huge quantities of wheat but relatively little for direct export. It also trades in iron ore and concentrates barley and oats and a variety of other primary products. Toronto has declined in relative importance, partly because of the increased size of ships deployed in international trade, and the heightened role of Montreal as the Atlantic terminus of the St Lawrence

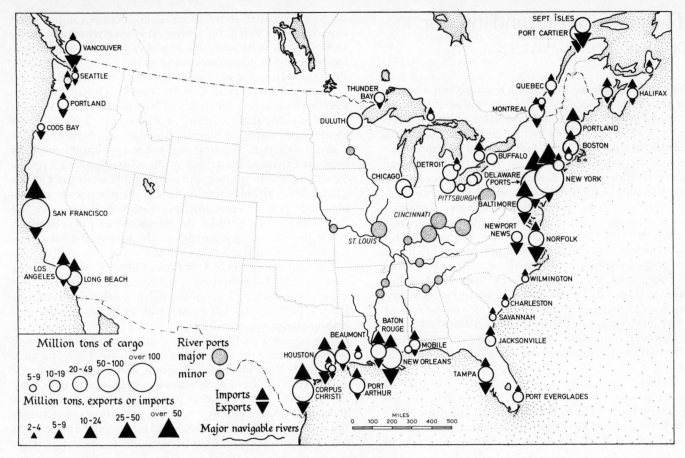

VANCOUVER
SEATTLE
PORTLAND
COOS BAY
SAN FRANCISCO
LOS ANGELES
LONG BEACH

THUNDER BAY
DULUTH
CHICAGO
DETROIT
BUFFALO
PITTSBURGH
CINCINNATI
ST. LOUIS

SEPT ÎSLES
PORT CARTIER
QUEBEC
HALIFAX
MONTREAL
PORTLAND
BOSTON
DELAWARE PORTS→
NEW YORK
BALTIMORE
NEWPORT NEWS
NORFOLK
WILMINGTON
CHARLESTON
SAVANNAH
JACKSONVILLE
TAMPA
PORT EVERGLADES

BATON ROUGE
BEAUMONT
MOBILE
HOUSTON
NEW ORLEANS
CORPUS CHRISTI
PORT ARTHUR

Million tons of cargo

River ports
major
minor

5-9 10-19 20-49 50-100 over 100

Million tons, exports or imports

2-4 5-9 10-24 25-50 over 50

Imports
Exports

Major navigable rivers

MILES
0 100 200 300 400 500

35 » The major coastal and interior ports of North America, 1974 figures

Seaway System. The other Lake ports deal largely with the movement of coal, iron ore, petroleum, timber and grain within the Great Lakes basin.

Despite recent developments in transportation the Mississippi-Missouri-Ohio system has not become outmoded as a cheap means of moving bulk commodities, and the great interior river ports are almost comparable, in tonnage handled, with many of the major seaports. Traffic is dominated by the upstream movement of oil and petroleum products from the extensive fields of Louisiana and Texas (cf. Map 22) to the industrial centres of the Midwest.

36 The St Lawrence Seaway

The St Lawrence Seaway-Great Lakes System links the Atlantic, the world's greatest trading ocean, with the rich continental heartland of North America. It is essentially a man-made waterway, for in its natural state the route was of limited value. Upstream from Quebec, the original head of navigation, were narrow, sand-choked channels; between Montreal and Kington the Lachine, Soulanges and International Rapids presented a succession of obstacles to navigation with a combined rise of 221 feet. Between Lakes Ontario and Erie stood the Niagara Falls; the passage to Lake Huron via the Detroit and St Clair Rivers needed constant dredging; commercial navigation was impossible before locks were constructed.

Improvements began early. The first series of small canals around the rapids at Sault Ste Marie was built in 1789, and locks with a depth of 11·5 feet were opened in 1855. The first Welland Canal around Niagara Falls was opened in 1829, and between 1845 and 1887 this 8-foot barge canal was improved to 14 feet. Shallow canals were built between Kingston and Montreal in 1848 and deepened in 1903. A larger Welland Canal was opened in 1932, and by the late 1940s the St Lawrence-Great Lakes route consisted of two well-developed 'ends', with a bottleneck in the middle. The channel to Montreal took vessels of 25,000 tons, and from Kingston to Duluth a continuous waterway with depths of 21 feet to 25 feet accommodated vessels of 20,000 tons. Between Kingston and Montreal the narrow canal system was barely navigable for vessels of 4,000 tons.

Since the end of the nineteenth century intermittent negotiation had been held between the United States and Canada for joint development of both navigation and hydro-electric power along the St Lawrence waterway that formed their common frontier. Each time that agreement was reached the resulting treaty failed to pass the United States senate. In 1951 the Canadian parliament established the St Lawrence Seaway Authority and passed the International Rapids Power Development Act, demonstrating that the Dominion was prepared to take unilateral action. Three years later, after intensive negotiations had resolved the political problems inherent in the scheme, the United States congress passed similar legislation. The main objectives were to improve navigation on the Great Lakes, clear the St Lawrence bottleneck, and exploit its hydro-electric potential. The first of the power facilities came into operation in 1958, and the Seaway officially opened in 1959.

Navigation channels had been deepened to provide a minimum 27-foot depth taking vessels of 25,000 tons. Construction costs amounted to $470 million, of which Canada bore 75 per cent. Tolls are divided between the two countries in proportion to the annual charges required to amortise the capital investment over fifty years and to meet operating and maintenance costs. The result is a waterway extending 2,300 miles from the Atlantic to the mid-continent. The industrial and agricultural heartland of North America is now accessible to ocean shipping, and trade throughout the region has grown steadily, primarily because of the lowering of freight costs: a ton of bulk cargo can now be moved from Chicago to Liverpool for less than the overland freight charges to traditional east-coast trans-shipment ports. The biggest limitation on growth is the winter freezing of the St Lawrence that usually closes the Seaway between December and April.

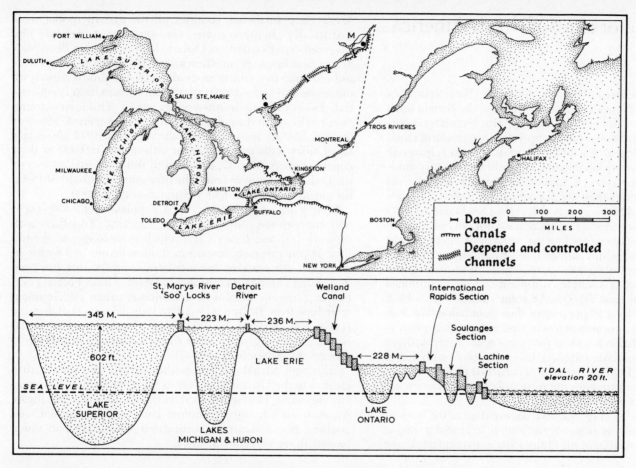

FORT WILLIAM

DULUTH

LAKE SUPERIOR

SAULT STE. MARIE

M

K

MILWAUKEE

LAKE MICHIGAN

LAKE HURON

TROIS RIVIERES

MONTREAL

CHICAGO

DETROIT

HAMILTON

KINGSTON

LAKE ONTARIO

HALIFAX

TOLEDO

LAKE ERIE

BUFFALO

BOSTON

NEW YORK

⊢ **Dams**
〰 **Canals**
≋ **Deepened and controlled channels**

0   100   200   300
MILES

St. Marys River
'Soo' Locks

Detroit River

Welland Canal

International Rapids Section

Soulanges Section

Lachine Section

345 M.

223 M.

236 M.

228 M.

602 ft.

LAKE ERIE

TIDAL RIVER elevation 20 ft.

SEA LEVEL

LAKE SUPERIOR

LAKES MICHIGAN & HURON

LAKE ONTARIO

36 » The St Lawrence Seaway–Great Lakes System

37 The major cities of North America

Urban sprawl has been one of the dominant characteristics of great cities in advanced industrial societies. In Britain such extended cities are called 'conurbations'; this term has no currency in the United States but an approximate equivalent exists in the 'urbanised area'. Each of these must contain at least one city of 50,000 or more inhabitants, and embraces the surrounding closely settled areas of adjacent counties; but unlike the British conurbations they are not defined by political boundaries. The United States census also recognises Standard Metropolitan Statistical Areas that are defined not only in terms of population but also according to criteria of metropolitan character and economic integration. Each SMSA includes either a core city of 50,000, or two cities, with contiguous boundaries forming a single community, with a combined population of at least 50,000. Adjacent counties are added, provided that at least 50 per cent of their population live at an urban density in contiguous townships, a significant proportion of the population has an employment relationship with the core city, and economic and social life is integrated with that of the city. In New England, because of particular historical problems, SMSAs are based not upon counties but upon cities and towns that meet equivalent criteria.

The use of the readily available county data as the basis of delimitation results in gross overdefinition, in spatial terms, of many of the great cities of the United States, particularly in the West. Here small-size counties on the eastern model were historically inappropriate for settlement needs. The Riverside-San Bernardino-Ontario SMSA, number 29 on Map 37, is a clear case in point: stretching 200 miles from east to west and 180 miles from north to south it consists almost entirely of mountain and semi-desert; significant urbanisation is concentrated in its extreme south-western corner. This is an extreme case, but many of the cities are similarly overdefined. Many of the 265 SMSAs recognised by the census in 1974 are in fact small cities with populations of only about 100,000 in their extended form. Map 37, designed to show the major cities of the United States, plots only the fifty most populated SMSAs, the smallest of which had a population of 766,000.

New York, with a 1974 SMSA population of 9,634,000, is still the primate city of North America. Together with Newark (15) and Jersey City, which is no longer in the top fifty, it contains over seventeen million people and forms an extended and massive metropolitan complex that has been designated a Standard Consolidated Area. 'Greater New York' lies in a region of almost continuous urban development stretching from Boston (6) south to Philadelphia (4), Baltimore (14) and Washington, DC (8). This urbanised north-east seaboard containing more than forty million people has been termed 'Megalopolis' (Map 47).

Although Megalopolis is without rival, two other urban clusters in the United States are as big as the largest European city regions. The south-western shore of Lake Michigan, focussed on Chicago, is almost completely urbanised, and contains two Standard Consolidated Areas each containing two or more vigorous SMSAs.

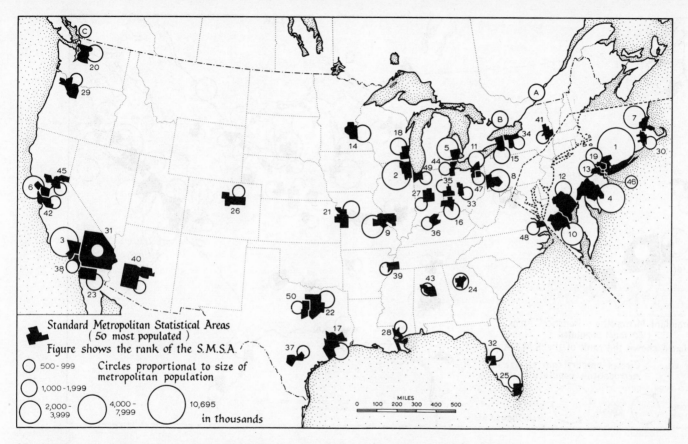

Standard Metropolitan Statistical Areas
(50 most populated)
Figure shows the rank of the S.M.S.A.

500 - 999

Circles proportional to size of
metropolitan population

1,000 - 1,999

2,000 - 3,999   4,000 - 7,999   10,695

in thousands

MILES
0 100 200 300 400 500

37a » The major standard metropolitan statistical areas of the USA, 1960, and the metropolitan cities
of Canada, 1961

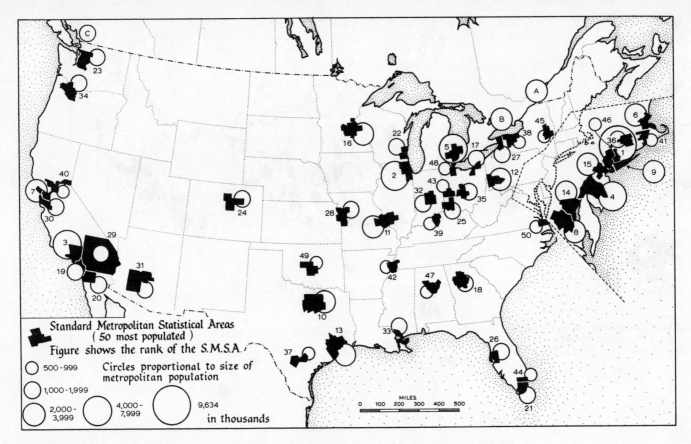

37b » The major standard metropolitan statistical areas of the USA, 1970, and the metropolitan cities of Canada, 1971

Another cluster of SMSAs with megalopolitan characteristics is centred on Los Angeles, includes most of southern California and had a 1974 population of 10·2 million. From Santa Barbara, which is too small for inclusion on Map 37, south to Los Angeles (3), through Anaheim (19) to San Diego (20), and inland to Riverside–San Bernardino–Ontario (29), urban growth has spread discontinuously. Urbanisation in southern California has been developing faster than along the north-eastern seaboard or in the Chicago region; the empty tracts between the constituent cities are being developed in the dispersed urban pattern that is California's distinctive contribution to the form of the modern city, though whether this represents the wave of the future for all modern societies or just a unique evolutionary cul-de-sac, dependent as it has been upon cheap petroleum, remains to be seen.

The Boston–Washington 'Megalopolis' together with the Chicago and Los Angeles urban clusters contain about 31 per cent of the population of the United States. Elsewhere there are great regional contrasts in the intensity of urbanisation. Megalopolis and Chicago represent the east–west ends of the Manufacturing Belt; between them lies a varied urban pattern. On the Appalachian coalfield the small town, even the mining village, is the dominant settlement form, and here only Pittsburgh (12) is of great rank. Along the shores of Lake Erie and southward into Ohio and Indiana, SMSAs group in an incipient megalopolis: most of these cities are growing so quickly that there are clear signs of fusion, for example Cleveland (17) with its southern satellites, into semi-continuous, economically integrated urban regions.

There is a visible western frontier of great city development, currently marked by Minneapolis–St Paul (16) and Kansas City (28). Beyond this only Denver (24) qualifies for inclusion until Phoenix (31), the eastern outlier of the West Coast cities, is reached. The 'Old South', also, has few of the top fifty major metropolitan areas: Norfolk (50), Memphis (42), Atlanta (18), Birmingham (47) and New Orleans (33). Around the periphery recent industrial growth has been reflected in massive urban expansion, particularly in Houston (13) and the twin cities of Dallas–Fort Worth (10), while the urban scene in Florida is dominated by Tampa–St Petersburg (26), Miami (21) and the adjacent city of Fort Lauderdale (44).

Over the last decade the increasing importance of southern cities that do not show on this scale of analysis has emerged, whether thriving college towns, smaller financial and commercial centres, or multicentred conurbations of the Carolinas, such as Greensboro–Winston-Salem. Together with the tourist and retirement cities of Florida and the boom cities of Texas such places are changing the face of urban America, indicating the loosening of the tight grip once held by the cities of the Manufacturing Belt. In an era of ever-increasing fuel bills for corporations and householders alike the lure of the 'sunbelt' is strong.

38 City growth in the USA

Population growth in the United States has become an entirely urban phenomenon. During the twenty years after 1950 the total population in the continental United States rose from 151 to 203 million; the farm population fell sharply from twenty-three to under ten million, whilst the rural component as a whole was virtually stable at fifty-four million. Growth was concentrated in metropolitan areas, where the population grew by 27 per cent during the 1950s, and by 17 per cent in the 1960s, compared to national growth rates of 19 per cent and 13 per cent. Significantly the 11 per cent and 7 per cent growth rates in the core cities were lower than the 47 per cent and 26 per cent increases in the suburbs over the two decades. Though the post-war boom of the 1950s was not maintained, much of the decrease in the 1960s may however be more apparent than real, at least for the suburbs, as growth spilled over into rural areas faster than they could be reclassified as urban.

Megalopolis (cf. Map 47) attracted a huge total increase but significantly less than its proportionate share. The growth rates of the New York and Boston metropolitan areas were sluggish: where Boston at least maintained an 8 per cent growth rate, New York's fell from 12 per cent to 5 per cent. Further south Philadelphia's 18 per cent fell to 11 per cent. Washington, DC however accelerated from 37 per cent to 39 per cent, indicating some slight shift in the centre of gravity of population within Megalopolis. Based upon the business of government, the federal capital has undergone a population boom. The Washington, DC's SMSA extends far byond the District of Columbia and the surrounding urbanised areas, so that suburban expansion is contained within the total figure. By contrast the decrease in Jersey City is given undue prominence by the underdefinition of its metropolitan area. The poor performance of north-eastern manufacturing towns reflects their problems of industrial decline. Hartford, without a textile tradition but based on insurance, was the only New England town with persistently strong growth. In the Pennsylvania mining and metallurgy towns, growth was even slower than in New England. Pittsburgh and Johnstown actually lost population; industrial Appalachia in general has one of the poorest records of urban growth in the United States.

Urban growth quickens further west. Many towns in the Great Lakes-Ohio River section of the manufacturing belt prospered, and achieved growth rates ranging from 20 per cent to 40 per cent during the 1950s, though these were generally lower during the 1960s. Metropolitan Chicago and the Detroit-Cleveland urban cluster made rapid progress; but beyond Chicago, urban growth was strongly localised in a few cities such as St Louis and Kansas City.

The South showed only limited evidence of the urban explosion that is said to be revolutionising the socio-economic structure of the region. A few southern cities grew very strongly, particularly Atlanta with growth rates of 40 per cent and then 37 per cent; many smaller towns have experienced substantial increases, such as Charlotte, North Carolina; but the states of Mississippi and Arkansas attracted little share of the total national increase in urban population. Explosive rates

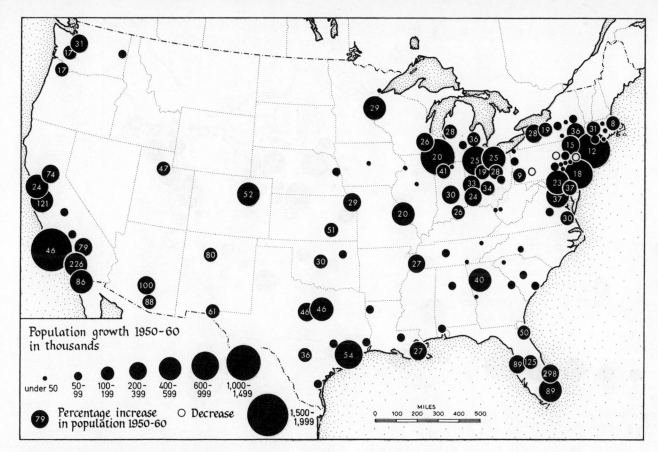

Population growth 1950–60
in thousands

under 50 50– 100– 200– 400– 600– 1,000–
         99   199   399   599   999 1,499

79 Percentage increase   ◯ Decrease
    in population 1950-60

1,500–
1,999

MILES
0 100 200 300 400 500

38a » City growth in the USA, 1950–60

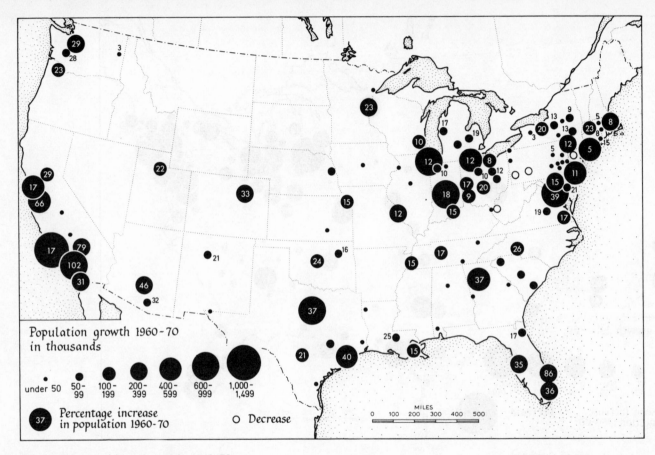

Population growth 1960-70
in thousands

under 50   50-   100-   200-   400-   600-   1,000-
           99   199   399   599   999   1,499

37   Percentage increase
     in population 1960-70   ○ Decrease

MILES
0   100 200 300 400 500

38b » City growth in the USA, 1960-70

were visible only in two atypical areas. Florida experienced an economic boom, partly because of the influx of tourists, retired people and Cuba's middle class; and several cities in Texas expanded by more than 45 per cent during the 1950s and retained high rates in the next decade.

In the Great Plains, the Mountain West and the South-West, significant urban expansion was confined to very few centres, but these have remarkable records. Phoenix, Tuscon and Albuquerque almost doubled during the 1950s. Phoenix's lower growth of a 'mere' 46 per cent during the 1960s was unmatched outside California and Florida. Salt Lake City and Denver developed at a slower pace throughout the two decades, but at rates few eastern cities could rival. Western urban expansion has in general been sustained by solid industrial progress, with the exception of such 'freak' economies as Reno and Las Vegas where prosperity has been based upon gambling. During the 1950s the Pacific North-West showed only steady, modest progress despite the prosperity and constant expansion of the aerospace industry based around Seattle. Despite subsequent industrial retrenchment growth has remained remarkably high during the 1960s. The most visible West Coast expansion during the two decades has been in California, particularly southern California. Neither the towns of the Central Valley nor even the cities of the San Francisco Bay area have matched the phenomenal and sustained expansion of the Los Angeles metropolitan region, which now challenges the supremacy of New York. Though the cluster of metropolitan areas based upon New York, with a consolidated population of over seventeen million, still outnumbers the Los Angeles cluster of just over ten million, the Los Angeles-based growth rate is now three times that of New York, and exceeds that of any other 'millionaire' city. In traditional terms Los Angeles is an urban absurdity, but its artificiality may allow greater flexibility in resolving the post-war problems of American society. Such flexibility however was based upon the twin assumptions of continued, limitless access to petroleum and water. Long-term survival will surely depend upon a successful adaptation to quite different conditions.

A comparison of Maps 38a and 38b illustrates certain basic trends throughout the two decades. The Manufacturing Belt has both lost ground to other areas, particularly the South-West, and has seen a shift of focus within the region. Elsewhere growth has been mainly in the 'sunbelt', stretching from Florida through the Gulf states across into the South-West, but even here the immense boom of places such as Fort Lauderdale, Florida and Anaheim, California that was such a statistical feature of the 1950s has shown a relative decline in the 1960s. With the exception of the Los Angeles region, growth in the sunbelt has still to produce a rival in absolute terms to the dominance of the Manufacturing Belt.

39 The distribution of rural population in the USA

The traditional agrarian and rural nature of American society has been reshaped during the twentieth century by the growth of an urban-industrial economy. When the first census was taken in 1790 only 5 per cent of the population was classified as urban; as late as 1840 a mere 10 per cent lived in towns; and in 1900, despite industrial expansion, six out of ten Americans were still country dwellers. Not until 1920 was there an urban majority, and then only by 2 per cent, but by 1960 the urban element had risen to almost 70 per cent, levelling out to 74 per cent over the next ten years. The surviving rural segment is not however synonymous with the farming population, for a distinction must be made between farm and 'non-farm' people, the latter consisting mainly of those living in agricultural, mining and industrial villages and, increasingly, commuters living in low densities in the rural 'exurban' zone beyond suburbia. By 1960, 75 per cent of the total rural population were classified as non-farm, rising to 82 per cent by 1970.

Maps 39a and 39b illustrate contrasts in the degree of 'ruralness' within the continental United States. Two measures are employed: the proportion of rural to total population is shown by a shading system on a state basis, and the proportion of the rural population actually engaged in farming is superimposed so that the heaviest pattern of shading identifies the most rural states.

In the North-East both indices of 'ruralness' are low, and few truly agrarian communities remain, as can be seen in the decline by 1970 of Vermont's relatively high ratio of rural to urban population in 1960. The 'rural' landscape that remains is the home of commuters, forestry workers, the retired, and tourist developers. In the South the high proportions of rural to urban populations that persist in the Carolinas are again frequently dominated by 'non-farm' people. West Virginia, Kentucky and Tennessee have slightly higher farm proportions but in the mountain areas of these states most 'rural' folk, in fact, live in depressed mining villages. Mississippi and Arkansas exhibit consistently high rural indices. On both maps Florida stands out as less rural than the rest of the South.

The urban dominated industrial Midwest continued to show moderate levels of 'ruralness' throughout the twenty-year period, but it is the prairie and high plains states, such as the Dakotas, that best illustrate the continued survival of agrarian America. The Spring Wheat Belt stands out as the rural heartland, but even in North Dakota, the most rural state, only one family in three lived on a farm by 1960, and only one in four by 1970. The northern tier of states in the Mountain West retains a significant rural character, but this is increasingly undermined by industrial development, ski resorts and dude ranches, particularly since 1970. Elsewhere in this region the farm population is thinly scattered across the semi-arid ranges, and is outnumbered even by the limited city growth.

Over the two decades portrayed here the steady drain of population from the farm areas has continued. Whether in the western mountains or the agricultural regions of the manufacturing belt the rural landscape is being filled by a reverse flow of urban people seeking benefits from rural living without having to engage in farming.

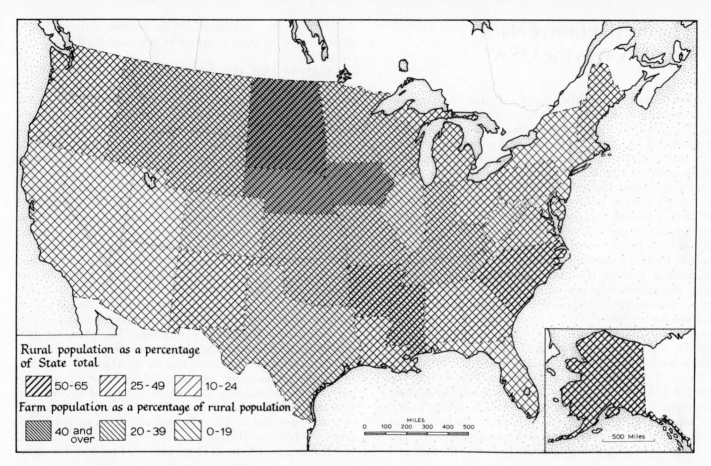

Rural population as a percentage
of State total

50-65   25-49   10-24

Farm population as a percentage of rural population

40 and
over   20-39   0-19

MILES
0   100 200 300 400 500

500 Miles

39 » The rural population of the USA, 1970

40 The distribution of black population in the USA

The Afro-American population remained relatively static and tied to the old cotton lands of the South until the First World War. Then, within a single generation, its distribution was transformed; a locational revolution took place that resulted, for example, in Illinois possessing a larger black population than Mississippi. This was an essential prelude to the social, economic and political revolution in black status that has made real, though painful, progress in recent decades. Before the Civil War, a limited number of southern blacks managed to settle in northern and midwestern states, and after the War a trickle of black people found their way out of the South; these, however, formed a minute percentage of the Afro-American population as a whole. The first major migration took place during the industrial boom of the First World War when northern manufacturers, deprived of their traditional supply of cheap immigrant labour, turned to the domestic reservoir of unskilled workers. Southern blacks went north in increasing numbers; the movement continued during the prosperous 1920s, waned during the depression, accelerated again during the Second World War, and continued after 1945 (cf. Map 41). In the 1940s blacks also began to break new ground by moving to the west coast, particularly into the industrial cities of southern California. By 1960 almost one million blacks lived in this region where, prior to 1940, there had been almost none. The great migration, pregnant with implications for the future of American society, had resulted in the creation of two radically different types of black community: southern rural and northern urban.

Already by 1960, as a result of the exodus, the urban black population had reached six million in the northern industrial states. This rose to nine million by 1970, now increasingly due to local natural increase rather than in-migration, and there are indications that such rapid increase is now levelling out. In their migrations blacks have been selective, moving chiefly to the great cities and those towns that have shown rapid industrial growth. Some medium-sized cities with expanding economies, such as Indianapolis and Cincinnati, were between 20 per cent and 30 per cent black by 1960. By 1970 Cincinnati's blacks made up over 27 per cent of a total city population that had declined by 10 per cent during the decade, illustrating yet again the white flight to the suburbs. But black migrants avoided towns with industrial problems or highly organised traditional industries, so that Pittsburgh and the Appalachian mining centres had relatively small Afro-American populations. However, in the decade 1960 to 1970 Pittsburgh's black minority rose from 16 per cent to 20 per cent, perhaps reflecting industrial regeneration in the area. The changing geographical distribution of the black population, from rural dispersion to urban concentration, transformed the traditional balance of American society. Inner cities have become predominantly black communities. By 1960 the centres of metropolitan Chicago and Philadelphia were 25 per cent black, rising to almost 35 per cent by 1970. Detroit rose from almost 30 per cent to 44 per cent, Baltimore from 35 per cent to 46 per cent, and Washington, DC from 55 per cent to 71 per cent during the

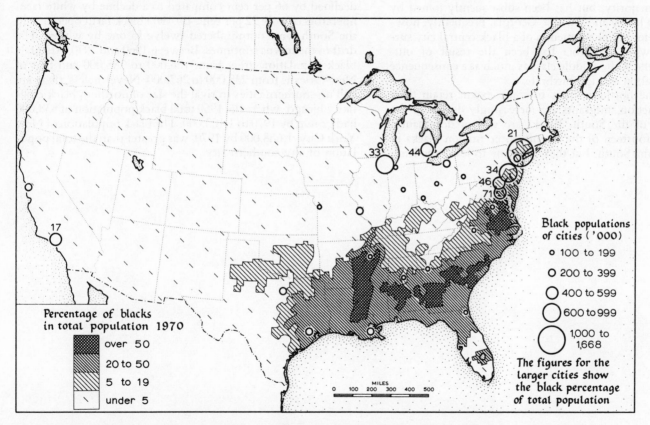

40 » The distribution of rural and urban black population in the USA. *The map is drawn to a county base; no attempt has been made to show the scattered counties in the Midwest where black population only slightly exceeds 5 per cent, 1970 figures*

same decade. The national capital was the first major city to have a black majority, but has been subsequently joined by Newark, New Jersey and Atlanta, Georgia. Frequently, however, this developing phenomenon of a black central city surrounded by white suburbia has been the result of out-migration by the white middle class as much as a consequence of black migration or high birthrate.

Although the northern cities to some extent retain their magnetic attraction, migrants are increasingly drawn to the growth cities of the South. Blacks are still predominantly southern, for fourteen of the twenty-three million blacks in 1970 lived in the South, but they continue to leave the land.

Between 1959 and 1969, black farm operators in the South declined by 66 per cent compared to a decline by white farm operators of only 22 per cent. By 1969 black farm operators in the South were outnumbered twelve to one by whites. The drift to the towns continues. Between 1960 and 1970, Atlanta's black population grew from 186,000 to 255,000 and that of New Orleans from 235,000 to 267,000. Nevertheless, there are still no southern cities to rival the size of northern black cities like Chicago, where the 1960 total black population of 838,000 had grown by 1970 to 1,103,000. The black population of New York City, 1,668,000 by 1970, was greater than the total population of any southern city.

41 The migration of black and white population in the USA

The American nation was born of migration; its nineteenth-century expansion embraced the greatest folk movement of modern times, and even the colonisation of the West and the elimination of the frontier could not stabilise a restless people. The spatial mobility of Americans continues, in response to rapidly changing patterns of economic and cultural opportunity. In the single year, 1963–4, no less than 19·6 per cent of the total population, some thirty-six million people, moved house; six million of these moved from one county to another within the same state, but another six million or 3·3 per cent of the population changed states. Over the five-year period 1965 to 1970 over 47 per cent, that is almost eighty-eight million people, moved house; 23 per cent, forty-three million, within the same county, and 18 per cent, 34·5 million, to a different county. Recent historical research into the experience of the urban North-East suggests that such a massive population turnover is a long-established feature of American life. During the 1960s the black population, though dispersing from its traditional southern homeland (cf. Map 40) was less mobile than the white majority: 4·4 per cent of the black population changed their county of residence in the year 1963 to 1964, compared with 6·9 per cent of the whites. However, between 1970 and 1973, 31·8 per cent of the white and 31·4 per cent of the blacks changed house. Blacks were moving house as frequently as whites.

Maps 41a and 41b show the geographical patterns of population change due to migration within the United States, by race, during the 1950s and the 1960s. Regionally coherent patterns emerge. The South, from the Carolinas to Oklahoma, including the Border States of West Virginia, Kentucky and Tennessee but excluding Maryland and Florida, was uniformly a region of outward migration by both blacks and whites during the 1950s. This drift from the South can be seen as a consequence of the reshaping of southern agriculture, although in West Virginia the mechanisation of the coal industry was a particular factor. In those southern states where industrial development has occurred, white out-migration in the 1950s was slight; in Texas, Virginia and Louisiana there was a small inward flow of whites, but the migration of blacks seemed to have been little retarded by such industrialisation. In the 1960s black out-migration persisted despite the increased prosperity of the South. The area of white influx however grew to include the Carolinas, Georgia and Mississippi, indicative of the modernisation of the South's economy. Florida has consistently departed from the general regional pattern; its agricultural and industrial prosperity, together with its attractiveness as a retirement and resort area, resulted in a large white increase over both decades, though a black inflow has not been maintained. The Florida population has also been joined by a massive inflow of Cuban exiles, particularly in the Miami area.

In the states of the manufacturing belt continued black in-migration is accelerating population growth and changing the racial composition of the region. Throughout the two decades the industrial states have been attracting black migrants, any white inflow being outweighed by that of the black. Some

117

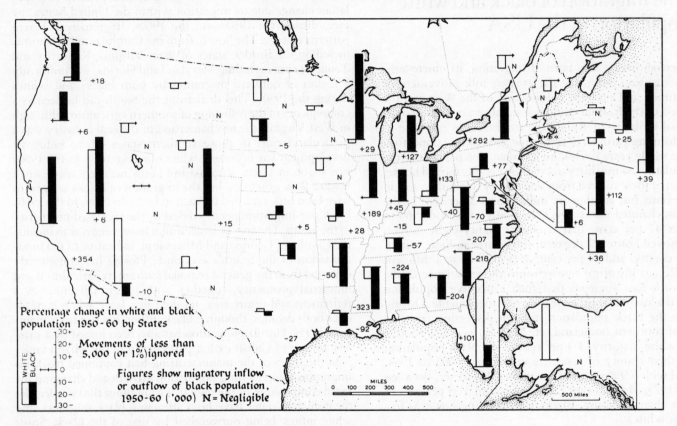

Percentage change in white and black
population 1950-60 by States

Movements of less than
5,000 (or 1%) ignored

Figures show migratory inflow
or outflow of black population,
1950-60 ('000)   N = Negligible

WHITE
BLACK

30+
20+
10+
0
10
20
30

MILES
0 100 200 300 400 500

500 Miles

41a » The migration of black and white population in the USA, 1950–60. *The columns show percentage change by migration, ignoring natural increase or decrease*

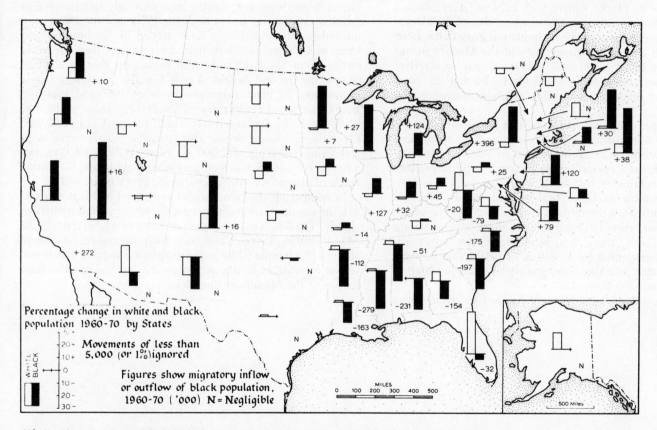

Percentage change in white and black population 1960-70 by States

20+
10+
WHITE
BLACK
0
10-
20-
30-

Movements of less than 5,000 (or 1%) ignored

Figures show migratory inflow or outflow of black population, 1960-70 ('000) N = Negligible

MILES
0 100 200 300 400 500

500 Miles

+10
+16
+272
+16
+7
+27
+124
+396
+30
+38
+120
+25
+79
+45
+32
+127
-14
-20
-79
-175
-112
-51
-197
-231
-279
-154
-163
-32

41b » The migration of black and white population in the USA, 1960–70. *The columns show percentage change by migration, ignoring natural increase or decrease*

states, such as Pennsylvania, have shown a persistent replacement of whites by blacks; others, such as New Jersey, show a white influx, but even this is only a quarter that of the blacks. Black settlement is greatest where industrial growth has been most rapid. In general the magnetism of the Manufacturing Belt is entirely black orientated. This trend may well reflect more the expectations of southern blacks leaving the rural South than any objective availability of labour-intensive jobs in the North.

A third type of migrational trend can be identified in the rural states of the northern Great Plains, reaching from Wisconsin to Nebraska and into the Mountain States of Montana and Idaho. This is a region of population loss by migration, chiefly of white families, for the black element has always been negligible. It represents classic rural depopulation on a regional scale, and a shift from the farm to cities outside the region. In Colorado, where there has been at least two decades of strong industrial growth, there has been significant white in-migration accompanied by an influx of blacks that is slight compared to that into the major industrial states but high in percentage terms.

The Pacific region as a whole continues to attract large numbers of migrants, particularly blacks. The Pacific North-West, however, has become relatively unattractive to white in-migration, and in both the 1950s and the 1960s only limited numbers of blacks have settled in Washington and Oregon. California has long been the 'promised land' for white settlers, and since the industrial expansion that accelerated during the Second World War it has also become a major destination for black migrants. Between 1950 and 1960 the state experienced a net inflow of 354,000 blacks, in contrast to New York, its leading rival, which received only 282,000. Over the following decade this situation was reversed with California receiving 272,000 to New York's 396,000; but whereas New York was losing its white population, California received almost six white settlers for every black arrival.

In comparing the two decades portrayed in Maps 41a and 41b the essential continuity across the whole period stands out clearly. The South still loses people, most of whom settle in the Manufacturing Belt or California. Such contrasts as do emerge suggest that it is the white population that is starting to respond to the increase in southern prosperity and the relative stagnation of the Manufacturing Belt.

42 and 43   The distribution and growth of urban population in Canada

The urban revolution that has so radically transformed the population structure of the United States has only recently affected Canada. At Confederation 80 per cent of the Canadian population was rural: only six towns had reached 25,000, and only a single city, Montreal, had passed 100,000. The urban and rural elements in Canada's population did not reach parity until the eve of the Second World War; even in 1941 the Dominion contained only twenty-one towns of more than 25,000 and eight cities of more than 100,000. Since 1945 the urban revolution has gained momentum, and, in 1971, 76 per cent of the population was classified as urban. However, the Canadian census includes population clusters of only 1,000 within this definition, and the genuinely urban status of many of these townships must be questionable. More significantly, 43 per cent of the total population in 1971 lived in, or around, towns of more than 25,000 and almost 27 per cent were contained in cities over 100,000. The two cities of metropolitan status in eastern Canada, Montreal and Toronto, alone contained one-fifth of the entire country's population in 1961, rising to a quarter by 1971. Together with Vancouver these three great cities contained 30 per cent of the entire population of Canada by 1971.

Urban growth has been very unevenly distributed throughout the country. In Newfoundland and the Maritimes there are only three cities of substantial size; each is the major port of its region but even the considerable growth of Halifax, the leading port of Atlantic Canada, was well below the national average during the boom times of the 1950s, and was halved, in percentage terms, during the 1960s. Relative urban stagnation in these provinces reflects their economic weakness and continued dependence on unrewarding agriculture.

Most of Canada's urban growth has been concentrated in the industrial heartland along the St Lawrence and in the Ontario peninsula. The two metropolitan centres, Montreal and Toronto, each exceed two million, and three other cities have about half a million. Quebec and Ontario are now urbanised provinces in which industry and commerce dominate both the economy and the employment structure, but within this urban core of Canada growth trends show strong intraregional contrasts. Montreal, the primate city of French-speaking Canada, continues to grow less rapidly than Toronto, although Quebec City has grown significantly over the past two decades. Kitchener, Hamilton, London and Windsor have become vigorous cities based upon flourishing industry and agriculture. The expansion of Ottawa, the national capital, reflects both the increased size and complexity of government and varied industrial development within the city. Quebec City, seat of the political ambitions of French-speaking Canada, enjoyed twice Ottawa's rate of growth during the 1960s, indicative of the new dynamism in Quebec Province.

Urban growth rates during the 1950s were highest in western Canada. Winnipeg alone among the prairie cities was of substantial size before the Second World War; other towns in the Prairie Provinces were merely regional marketing, distribution and service centres. The enormous expansion of oil

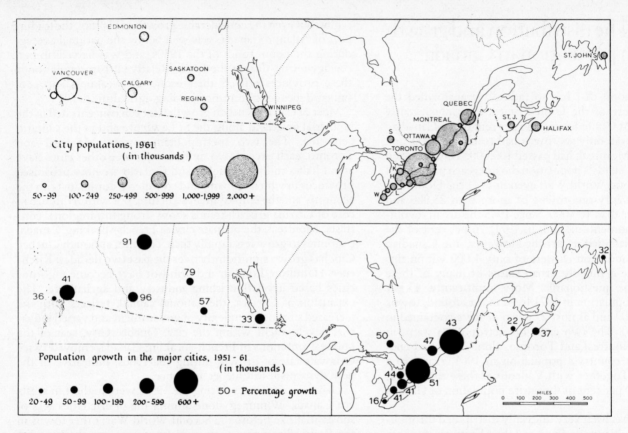

42a » The distribution of urban population in Canada. *StJ = Saint John, K = Kitchener, H = Hamilton, L = London, W = Windsor, S = Sudbury, V = Victoria*

42b » City growth in Canada, 1951–61

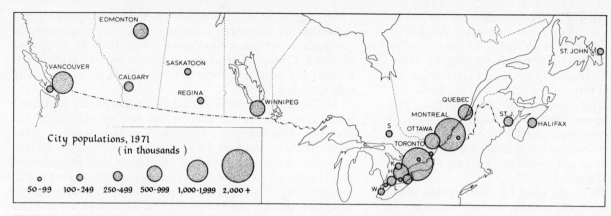

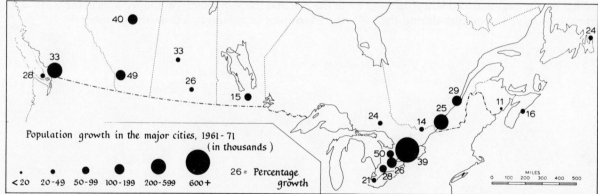

43a » The distribution of urban population in Canada. *StJ = Saint John, K = Kitchener, H = Hamilton, L = London, W = Windsor, S = Sudbury, V = Victoria*

43b » City growth in Canada, 1961–71

and natural gas (cf. Map 23), has transformed the urban economy of the region. Alberta has dominated the prairie hydrocarbon industry, with the result that Edmonton grew by 91 per cent during the 1950s and 40 per cent during the 1960s, and Calgary by 96 per cent and 49 per cent. Even though the rate of increase slowed throughout Canada in the 1960s, the western cities still generally outpaced those in the East. The major cities of Saskatchewan – Regina and Saskatoon – showed relatively inferior rates of growth, but far exceeded the national average for large metropolitan centres. Winnipeg, deriving little direct benefit from oil and natural gas, has languished and may be overtaken by Edmonton.

Urban growth on the Pacific coast has been modest compared to expansion of the prairie cities, due to the absence of any extraordinary stimulus to the regional economy: metropolitan Vancouver grew by 'only' 41 per cent during the 1950s, and by 33 per cent in the 1960s. This was phenomenal expansion by European standards, and very respectable in comparison with most American cities (cf. Map 38); its limited impact in Canadian terms underlines the rapidity with which Canada has been transformed from a rural to an essentially urban society.

Any comparison between the two decades here portrayed needs care, for the slowing in the rate of expansion still involved often massive growth with all its associated problems. At the national level a comparison between the various centres of growth is revealing. Although the constitutional clash between Quebec and Ottawa may seem paramount, this struggle may in fact obscure the increasingly bi-nodal nature of Canadian society, centred around the Toronto-Montreal axis in the east and the Vancouver-Winnipeg axis in the west, with the Maritimes increasingly left on the periphery.

44 and 45 The distribution of rural population and ethnic groups in Canada

Map 44 draws a primary distinction between areas of continuous and discontinuous rural settlement in Canda, and also gives a measure of density. Even discontinuous settlement patterns contain locally 'high' densities of up to forty per square mile: values above this usually indicate the presence of towns and cities, but the scale of the map does not allow such urban breaks within the spread of rural population to be shown. Pioneer settlements form isolated pockets that are also occasionally of 'high' density.

Atlantic Canada is a region of early settlement but environmental poverty, for agricultural opportunity has always been limited. Farms cluster thickly in the valleys and along the coast; in these fertile areas agriculture is intensive, but living standards are generally low by North American values, and both rural depopulation and land abandonment are serious problems. From the estuarine lowlands of the St Lawrence to the Ontario peninsula stretches a region of continuously dense rural population and highly productive farming (cf. Map 14b). Although rural densities are no higher than in the more limited agricultural areas in the Maritimes, the land supports a stable rural society enjoying a relatively high standard of living.

In Quebec and Ontario the edge of the Shield broadly marks the limit of dense, continuous rural settlement, although strong salients reach deeply into the Shield in the Ottawa and Saguenay valleys. From the main mass of rural population in southern Quebec and Ontario broken ribbons of settlement cross the Shield along the lines of the major railways (cf. Map 32), where mining and scattered industrial activity based on pulp and paper have stimulated local farming. In the fertile clay belt straddling the Quebec-Ontario border these railway ribbons thicken to form one of the most remote rural population clusters in eastern Canada.

Rural population densities in the Prairie Provinces are not simply related to contrasts in soil fertility. Highly productive black and chestnut soils support only a low average density because of intensive mechanisation of commercial wheat farming. The poorer soils of the forest fringe flanking the Wheat Belt are associated with higher densities for although much of the land is still uncleared, the cultivated area is devoted to labour-intensive mixed farming (cf. Map 14a). Beyond the edge of continuous settlement are scattered pioneer communities: one well-defined chain reaches along the Nelson River from the mining towns of Manitoba to Hudson Bay, others have grown around isolated mines in north central Saskatchewan and Alberta. The major outlier of continuous rural population lies in the Peace River country of Alberta and British Columbia, opened to settlement as recently as the 1920s.

The locational pattern of West Coast rural population resembles that of the Maritimes since it is largely confined to coastal strips and interior valleys. It is, however, more discontinuous; although locally dense in the Okanagan and lower Fraser lowlands, it is sparse and scattered in the valleys further north, forming communities little removed from the pioneer stage.

125

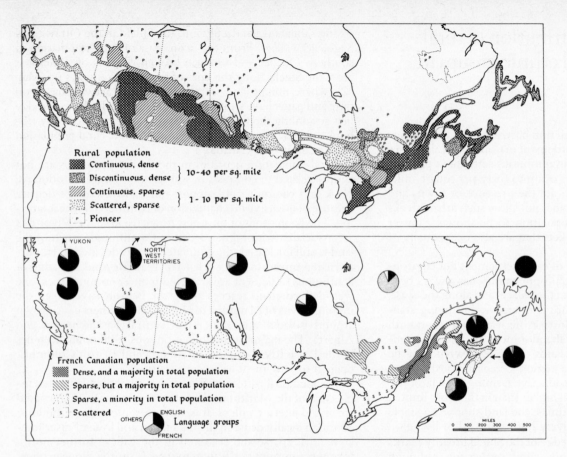

Rural population

Continuous, dense ⎫
Discontinuous, dense ⎬ 10-40 per sq. mile
Continuous, sparse ⎫
Scattered, sparse ⎬ 1-10 per sq. mile
P Pioneer

YUKON
NORTH
WEST
TERRITORIES

French Canadian population

Dense, and a majority in total population
Sparse, but a majority in total population
Sparse, a minority in total population
s Scattered

OTHERS ENGLISH
FRENCH Language groups

MILES
0 100 200 300 400 500

44 » The distribution of rural population in Canada, 1970
45 » Ethnic composition of the Canadian population by language groups, 1970

The most developed and agriculturally productive areas in the hinterland of Vancouver (cf. Map 14a) contain the most significant nuclei of thickly clustered rural population.

French Canada is one of North America's major culture regions, as distinctive in language and custom as the Latin American civilisation south of the Rio Grande. Map 45 illustrates the distribution by province of Canadian ethnic groups, with particular reference to the French Canadians. The cultural hearth of French Canada lies clearly in the St Lawrence lowlands, where French-speaking elements are densely grouped and form a majority of the total population. Important extensions are found in the Saguenay valley, around Lake St John and along the New Brunswick coast.

Throughout Canadian history French explorers and settlers have been adventurous and tenacious pioneers, and most of the population of the Shield, in 'British' Ontario as well as in 'French' Quebec, are of French descent and culture. The considerable areas of French-Canadian settlement in the Prairie Provinces reflect early penetration by trappers and traders into the empty Canadian west, but most of the French families of western Canada are recent migrants, attracted to the virgin lands from overcrowded farms in the St Lawrence valley. This movement was not slowed by the rapid industrialisation of Quebec that has converted the French-Canadian population from a dominantly rural community of peasant farmers to an increasingly urbanised society.

In addition to the dominant Anglo-Saxon and French elements other ethnic groups are found in significant numbers, particularly in the Prairie Provinces. Canada shared in the mass migration from Europe in the late nineteenth and early twentieth centuries, and Germans, Scandinavians and eastern Europeans have produced a variegated ethnic pattern to the north as well as south of the 49th parallel. Many of these still live in culturally distinct communities, and in Saskatchewan they form a majority of the total population. Peoples of Indian and Eskimo descent dominate the population in the North West Territories, and are a significant minority in the Yukon.

46 The American city: Chicago

Chicago, the metropolis of the mid-continent, embodies many of the characteristics that have given a distinctive quality to the North American urban landscape. The gridiron street pattern, first employed in William Penn's Philadelphia at the end of the seventeenth century, was adopted for the towns established in the expanding West, and the 'block' system became one of the most pronounced features of urban development. As with other major cities Chicago has become overlaid with subsequent transport systems, particularly the vast freeway network that criss-crosses both the city and its suburbs.

The modern city of Chicago was created by the railroads. Reaching into the Midwest in the 1850s they enabled the town of Chicago to attain pre-eminence in the upper Mississippi valley, capitalising upon its waterfront position and with access to a massive and developing agricultural hinterland. Into its stockyards flowed the cattle of the Great Plains, into its storage elevators poured the grain of the Wheat Belts, and the city became a centre of milling, meat-packing and agricultural machinery. Clothing and furniture industries followed, and by the end of the nineteenth century Chicago had become a manufacturing centre of world importance. The establishment of the Gary steelworks across the Indiana line in 1906 further confirmed the new industrial strength of the region.

Traditional methods of transportation continue to provide vital links between the city and its hinterland. Railroads retain much of their importance for freight haulage; the opening of the St Lawrence Seaway permits access both to world markets and foreign raw materials (cf. Map 36). New forms of transportation have merely reinforced Chicago's role, whilst involving often massive reorganisation of land use within the city itself. Earlier it became a railroad hub; since 1945 it has become one of the focal points of the interstate highways system, and a major trucking centre; developments in air transport have made the city's O'Hare International airport the busiest in North America. Such developments involve massive commitments of land outside the congested inner city, part of a re-orientation of Chicago's development into suburban locations. This metropolitan expansion affects the city's tax base and aggravates the traditional jurisdictional problems relating to the provision of essential services. As in other US metropolitan areas there is a complex mosaic of often overlapping authorities and special agencies involved in the provision of public facilities.

The heart of the traditional American city is the 'downtown' area, or Central Business District (CBD), into which business, commerce and finance crowd according to principles of mutual attraction. In Chicago this is the historic 'Loop', once encircled by an elevated urban railroad. The CBD is dominated by skyscraper offices, department stores and hotels catering increasingly to the convention and conference trade-buildings that rise high to offset the high cost of centrally located land. The continued magnetism of established business associations within this area has enabled the Loop to retain its traditional role as the commercial core of the entire metropolitan region, despite the development of satellite centres in the suburban

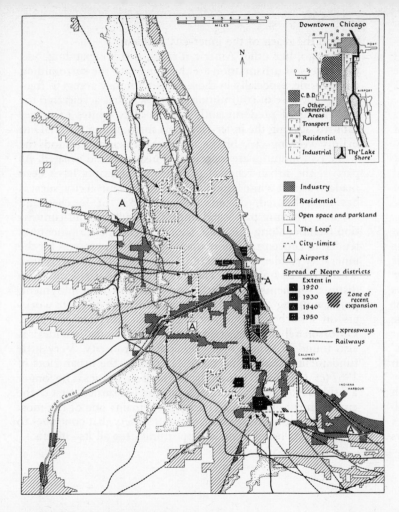

Downtown Chicago

C.B.D.

Other
Commercial
Areas

Transport

Residential

Industrial   The 'Lake
Shore'

Industry

Residential

Open space and parkland

L   'The Loop'

City-limits

A   Airports

Spread of Negro districts

Extent in
1920
1930
1940   Zone of
1950   recent
expansion

Expressways

Railways

fringe. Industry, however, has increasingly found the congested inner-city areas unsuitable for new and extensive plant that require ease of access to the freeway system, although the city has tried to provide suitable new facilities as the stockyards and railroad yards are cleared.

Like many American cities Chicago is the product of rapid and ruthless urbanisation between 1860 and 1920. A tide of European immigrants poured into the city after 1880, concentrating in the inner suburbs and providing cheap and unskilled labour for industrial expansion. Their low-cost and outdated housing deteriorated quickly, leaving a legacy of dilapidation that now presents massive problems of urban renewal. These European immigrants at first formed distinct ethnic communities and, although most people became assimilated into the life of the city, many of the loyalties towards particular neighbourhoods and communities remain. Also, since about 1910, Chicago has been one of the major destinations for the great waves of black migration from the rural South (cf. Maps 40 and 41); and from the original small nuclei of blacks a major ghetto has spread rapidly southwards from the Loop along the line of the elevated railroad that blighted the environment along its track. The strength of prejudice has made the 'walls' of the ghetto even higher than those faced by the European immigrant, and the process of assimilation has consequently been slower. Furthermore the supply of unskilled jobs, which did at least permit the European immigrant to enter the job market, has progressively diminished as mechanisation takes over and factories are built along the suburban freeways beyond the reach of the inner-city resident.

Chicago, like other American cities, is still expanding, and the fingers of urbanisation are thrusting into the surrounding countryside, especially in those areas with easy access to freeways. The ease of commuting by freeway has accelerated the movement of predominantly middle-class whites to newer suburbs, leaving the inner-city areas surrounding the CBD to mainly working-class blacks, from whose neighbourhoods the white communities are increasingly insulated and isolated. As part of the urban-renewal programme attempts have been made to attract white families back into the central city; success has been limited, despite the attractions of beaches and marinas, pleasure parks and impressive cultural and convention facilities along the 'Lake Shore'. Recent development has tended to concentrate more upon job-creation projects for the inner-city residents than attempts to redress the racial balance within the city at large. The city is thus polarised into two distinct segments, the black inner zones of unemployment, public housing and poverty, and an outer belt of white workers, in suburban homes with access to American affluence. Unfortunately this geography of America's unrealised ideals is also found in almost every other American city. Very little fundamental change has taken place since the urban riots of 1967 (cf. Map 53). Though the plight of such cities is no longer a fashionable pre-occupation as interest has turned, first to the environment and then to energy, it remains one of the most pervasive problems for an American society that continues to articulate its belief in equal opportunity for all its citizens.

47 Megalopolis

The north-eastern seaboard, from Boston to Washington, DC, is the most heavily urbanised part of the United States: over forty million people, almost 20 per cent of the total population, occupy less than 2 per cent of the land area. The designation 'Megalopolis' was first applied by Jean Gottmann in recognition that this area is important, not so much for the size of its population or for the concentration of metropolitan areas so close together, but because the massive degree of interaction between the various centres is such that they form a new type of urban structure, whose existence could be defined in terms of certain criteria of urban intensity and functional linkage. Map 47 departs from Gottmann by including in Megalopolis only those contiguous counties along the north-eastern seaboard with a 1970 population density of 150 or more per square mile. Within this area degrees of urbanisation are shown in order to correct the impression that Megalopolis is one continuous 'conurbation', for beyond the cities and their suburbs lie dependent rural or semi-rural zones. Despite the general intensity of urbanisation, the major impression of the landscape from the air remains one of great cities surrounded by great forests.

The inherent dynamism of the region stems from its polynuclear cores at Boston, New York, Philadelphia, Baltimore and Washington, DC. With the exception of Washington, these are great port-cities that since colonial times have been engaged in intense rivalry for trade and industry. Here lay the economic hinge of North America, facing outwards towards Europe but acting at the same time as the base for continental expansion. Apart from its continuing financial, commercial and industrial role Megalopolis has historically been a centre of political and cultural activity that has helped to shape the patterns of American civilisation.

The region is afflicted by most of the problems of intense urbanisation. Its economic function has suffered from the obsolescence of many early industries, but growth has recently been re-invigorated by new industrial technologies (cf. Maps 29 to 30). In law, commerce and finance its continued dominance is reflected in the upsurge in office construction in the Central Business Districts, such as New York's World Trade Center. The major problems of the residential function of the various metropolitan areas lie in urban sprawl and the related issue of urban deterioration. Suburban growth around each metropolis is engulfing rural land as the more affluent sections of the population have abandoned all but certain select quarters of the inner cities, which consequently have large areas of deteriorating slums (cf. Map 46). Urban renewal is designed partly to attract middle- and upper-income residents back from the suburbs, for without them the financial base of the heavily urbanised areas must be uncertain. Cities are often in debt, and New York's situation has been perilous for too long. Traffic circulation also presents local, state and federal authorities with enormous problems, for Megalopolis continues to strangle itself with a surfeit of trucks and automobiles: the excellent regional turnpike and interstate highway systems permit easy inter-city movement, but also stimulate chronic

131

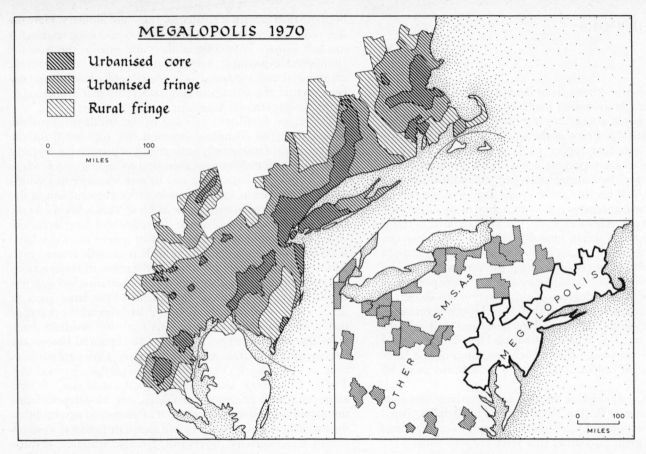

MEGALOPOLIS 1970

Urbanised core
Urbanised fringe
Rural fringe

0   100
MILES

OTHER S.M.S.As

MEGALOPOLIS

0   100
MILES

47 » Megalopolis: the urbanisation of the north-eastern seaboard

congestion within the cities and even the major highways become clogged at peak periods. Attempts to alleviate the congestion by building even more freeways are increasingly resisted by those neighbourhoods in the path of further construction. A by-product of high traffic densities is aggravation of the high level of air pollution created by concentrated industrial and residential buildings. This pollution, together with despoliation of waterways by industrial and human waste, has reached such proportions that the quality of the whole urban environment is threatened.

Although outpaced in metropolitan growth by other regions (cf. Map 38) Megalopolis is still expanding, both by intensification within established urbanised areas and by a process of peripheral accretion. The inset on Map 47 indicates the relationship of Megalopolis to the vigorous cities of the interior, and the possibility of eventual coalescence to form a gigantic super-Megalopolis around northern Appalachia, perhaps eventually linking up with Chicago to encompass the whole of the Manufacturing Belt (cf. Map 38). The question arises whether the United States has the combination of technological resources and political will to impose acceptable solutions, whether public or private, before such a massive agglomeration becomes too unwieldy for coherent management. Further growth may have to take new forms for the present structure, like much of American life, is based upon the promise of continued, cheap petroleum. In an era of energy shortage the great urban complexes of Megalopolis, like other metropolitan areas within the United States, may have to undergo profound adaptation if the present ingredients of American urban civilisation are to be continued.

48 The recreational West

Since they were first opened in the 1820s the lands west of the Mississippi have offered new economic opportunities to successive generations of Americans. The Great Plains and fertile intermontane and coastal valleys saw the development of productive agriculture (cf. Map 13); the vast open ranges encouraged sheep and cattle rearing (cf. Maps 18 to 19); the mountain forests provided lumber, and even many of the deserts and badlands were found to contain great mineral and oil resources (cf. Maps 20 to 22, 26). With the growth of western cities and the expansion of western industry (cf. Maps 27 to 30, 37 to 38), westward migration has continued (cf. Map 41). However, through a combination of geographical factors and historical accident, much open land remains, and the region has become one of the great vacationlands of North America.

Almost 34 per cent of the total land area of the United States is still in federal ownership. The highest regional percentage lies in the Mountain West (56·32 per cent); in the Pacific West 45·99 per cent is publicly owned, but federal lands in other census regions (cf. Map 49) nowhere exceed 7 per cent. Responsibility is largely vested in the Department of the Interior, which was established in 1849 and gradually embraced a multitude of special bureaux dealing with particular problems. From the beginning it included the General Land Office, now the Bureau of Land Management, with exclusive jurisdiction for the management of over 453 million acres, mostly in the eleven western states and Alaska. The Bureau of Sport, Fisheries and Wildlife is responsible for preserving and enhancing water resources for sport fishing, and for the protection of rare wildlife species such as the whooping crane, the American bald eagle and the buffalo. The National Wildlife Refuge System embraces twenty-eight million acres throughout the nation, including large reserves in the West.

The general concern of the Department with conservation of natural resources finds most visible expression in the activities of the National Park Service. The world's first national park was established under the authority of the Department in 1872: focussed on Yellowstone Lake and the valley of the Yellowstone River in Wyoming it extends into adjacent parts of Idaho and Montana. Its 3,472 square miles contain canyons, plateaux and mountains of outstanding natural beauty. After Yellowstone other parks were designated, including Grand Teton, Glacier, Yosemite and Olympic; the most recent is the 58,000 acre Redwood National Park in California that should ensure the survival of some of the coastal Sequoia. The National Park Service was created in 1916 to administer the parks for the enjoyment of the public whilst conserving natural flora and fauna. More than 216 million people annually visit the twenty-nine million acres of the National Park System and, despite serious overcrowding at popular parks such as Yosemite, the conservation programme has been conspicuously successful. The National Forests are controlled by the Department of Agriculture, but the simultaneous policy of conservation and utilisation has been equally successful.

A major division of the Interior Department is the Bureau of Indian Affairs with jurisdiction over Indian reservations,

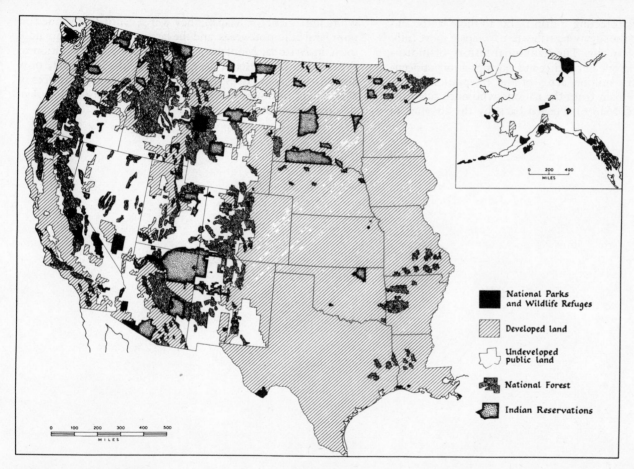

National Parks
and Wildlife Refuges

Developed land

Undeveloped
public land

National Forest

Indian Reservations

48 » The recreational West

responsibility for protecting Indian rights to these lands, and the task of helping the surviving tribes to participate more fully in modern American life. The traditional history of Indian-white relations was one of conflict and expropriation: concentrated on the fifty million acres of the reservations, only 437,000 Indians remain from the nations who once ruled the entire country (cf. Map 6). Pushed back by the advance of white settlement (cf. Map 8), they were eventually secluded on poor land in remote areas, and the largest reservations are now those in Arizona, Montana and South Dakota. In addition to the economic benefits of the tourist trade the Indians are now also sharing in revenues from the mineral and oil resources of their lands, although not without lengthy and often violent disagreements over respective treaty rights.

49 The census regions of the USA: population and revenue

The Constitution of the United States, ratified in 1789 and subsequently amended only twenty-six times, requires a census of the population to be taken every ten years. The primary purpose was to establish a basis for apportionment of members of the house of representatives among the states, but the statistics gathered have always been of social and economic as well as political utility. The first census was taken in 1790, and the decennial sequence has since been unbroken. Until the establishment of a permanent Bureau of the Census in 1902 responsibility was vested in temporary organisations; the Bureau, with a continuing responsibility, has expanded the scope of its operations and developed highly skilled techniques for the collection and analysis of basic data.

In the course of its work more sophisticated definition has been given to the regions of the United States that were historically described in loose geographical terms. Map 49 locates the census regions, gives their estimated 1974 population and indicates regional wealth in terms of *per capita* revenue of state and local governments. Map 50, in contrast, shows the distribution of wealth on a state basis using an index of family income. Although taxation needs and policies differ widely from state to state and region to region, and must be related to factors such as the intensity of urbanisation (cf. Maps 37, 39) and changing population characteristics (cf. Maps 40 and 41), a rough correlation can be seen between the *per capita* revenue of

state and local government shown on Map 49 and the family-income index employed on Map 50. Both regions of the old South, the South Atlantic and East South Central, are revealed as areas of low income in both personal and governmental terms. Relative poverty in the Dakotas is partly concealed on Map 49 by the inclusion of neighbouring and more prosperous states in the regional definition.

The United States has a federal form of government, but it would be incorrect to assume that the functions and responsibilities of the national government are entirely distinct and separate from those of the states. In addition to those areas such as foreign policy and national defence in which it has clear and absolute authority, the federal government has also been assumed to have wide-ranging domestic responsibilities in terms of the 'general welfare' and other such clauses of the constitution. The result has been that the direct influence of the federal government is felt in most sectors of public life, and over 17 cents of each federal tax dollar is paid back to state and local governments. The federal contribution reaches a peak of 33·7 per cent in Alaska, dropping to 14·8 per cent in Indiana. The federal percentage contribution to state budgets and hence to the regional economies has shown a fairly consistent upward trend during the past decade, reflecting the generally increased level of federal activity in social and economic programmes. Federal grants are made for a variety of specific purposes under the main headings of public welfare, highways, education and social insurance administration. Specific allocations that demonstrate the pervasive nature of federal activity include watershed protection and flood prevention, waste-treatment works and pollution control, urban renewal, economic oppor-

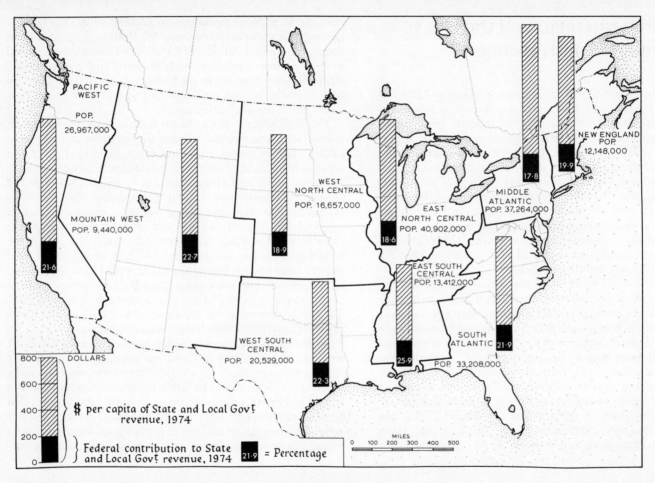

PACIFIC
WEST

POP.
26,967,000

21·6

MOUNTAIN WEST
POP. 9,440,000

22·7

WEST
NORTH CENTRAL

POP. 16,657,000

18·9

EAST
NORTH CENTRAL
POP. 40,902,000

18·6

MIDDLE
ATLANTIC
POP. 37,264,000

17·8

19·9

NEW ENGLAND
POP.
12,148,000

EAST SOUTH
CENTRAL
POP. 13,412,000

25·9

WEST SOUTH
CENTRAL
POP. 20,529,000

22·3

SOUTH
ATLANTIC

POP. 33,208,000

21·9

800 DOLLARS

600

400

200

0

$ per capita of State and Local Gov̧t
     revenue, 1974

} Federal contribution to State
  and Local Gov̧t revenue, 1974   **21·9** = Percentage

MILES
0   100 200 300 400 500

49 » The census regions of the USA: population and revenue, 1974

tunity programmes, hospital construction, maternal and child welfare and public assistance. The extent of federal aid in any region therefore reflects the social and economic composition of its population. In general the federal contribution is highest in rural areas that in national terms are the least prosperous; contributions in these areas are also enhanced by large conservation and natural resource programmes.

50 Poverty and wealth in the USA

The great wealth of the United States is unevenly distributed by class, by race and by region. In 1959 the average income of the poorest fifth of American families was $1,473, that of the richest fifth $12,293. By 1969 the gap had widened, $2,951 to $21,461. The average family income among blacks in 1959 was $3,463, among white $6,275; by 1969 a wide gap still existed, but it had narrowed, $7,255 compared to $10,953. Over the decade Alaska remained the state with the highest median family income, $7,305 rising to $12,441, whereas Mississippi remained the poorest, $2,884 rising to $6,068. It should be remembered that real income, though rising over the decade, was not as high as the figures might appear to indicate, for inflation reduced the spending power of the dollar by almost a quarter.

Maps 50a and 50b illustrate various criteria of prosperity in the United States. First, states are classified into four equal groups, or quartiles, on the basis of median family income. Averages are, however, often misleading and disguise the extent of poverty; a second measure is therefore incorporated: the percentage of families with income below an officially designated absolute minimum. Since the federal government defines poverty in terms of the family's most basic, immediate needs, these percentages represent people living in abject poverty. Further to these criteria, on Map 50a areas of local or regional high unemployment, designated as poverty areas by the Area Redevelopment Administration in 1961, are shown; Map 50b shows those six areas subsequently designated Economic Development Regions in 1965 in recognition that their economic and social problems required long-term, comprehensive planning and co-operative effort.

The South is clearly defined: every traditional 'cotton state' had a 1959 median family income below $4,600, and in almost all of them at least a quarter of the families had incomes below the federal minimum. The condition was particularly acute in Mississippi; elsewhere in the nation, even the low-income states of the Dakotas were significantly better off. Though conditions improved throughout the 1960s the South still stands out as having the largest proportion of its population living in abject poverty, though the High Plains again illustrate that, according to the criteria of 'ruralness' displayed on Map 39, states in the lowest income quartile are also the most rural. The designation of the Upper Great Lakes Economic Development Region, spreading across three states in the upper quartile in 1969, highlights the often great disparity within states that are either unable or unwilling to redevelop areas remote from the regions of affluence.

The largest concentration of wealthier families is found in the states of the Manufacturing Belt and the Pacific West. Even these states contain major depressed areas where unemployment reflects economic change. Industrial America presents a mosaic of poverty and prosperity: manufacturing states of high general income contain pockets of serious unemployment, located mostly in cities where particular industries are decen-

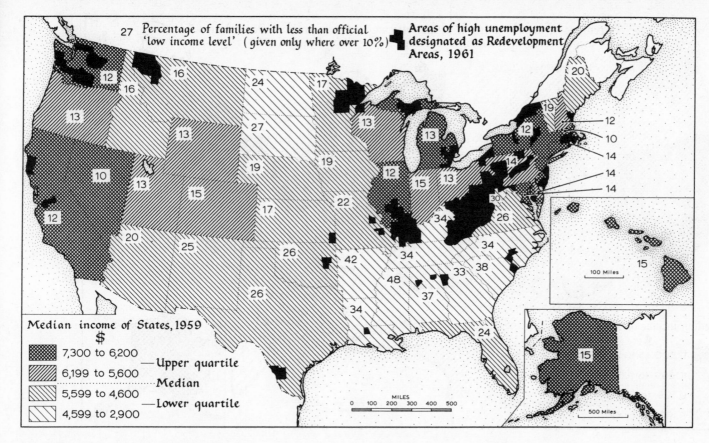

27 Percentage of families with less than official 'low income level' (given only where over 10%)

Areas of high unemployment designated as Redevelopment Areas, 1961

Median income of States, 1959
$

7,300 to 6,200	—Upper quartile
6,199 to 5,600	—Median
5,599 to 4,600	—Lower quartile
4,599 to 2,900	

50a » Poverty and wealth in the USA, 1959

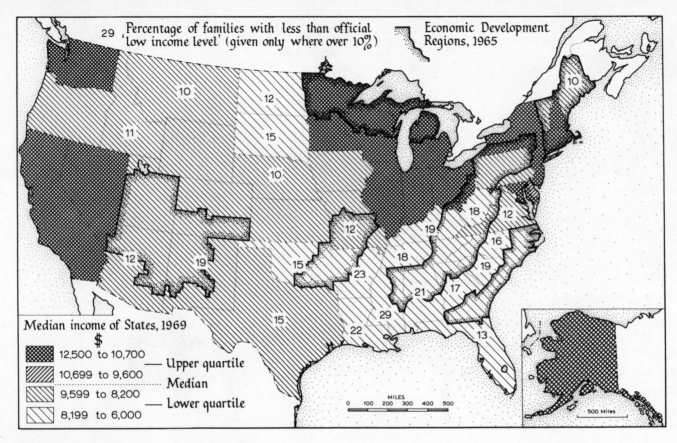

29 Percentage of families with less than official 'low income level' (given only where over 10%)

Economic Development Regions, 1965

Median income of States, 1969

$

12,500 to 10,700 — Upper quartile

10,699 to 9,600 ···· Median

9,599 to 8,200 — Lower quartile

8,199 to 6,000

MILES
0 100 200 300 400 500

500 Miles

50b » Poverty and wealth in the USA, 1969

tralising, declining or reducing their needs through automation: Detroit, Pittsburgh and the New England textile towns illustrate these situations. Such urban-industrial unemployment tends to be selective by race, and is invariably highest among blacks and Puerto Ricans. The elimination of many menial and manual jobs traditionally held by lower-income blacks, often recently arrived from rural poverty, has raised the unemployment rate in some black ghettos to 25 per cent. Although the proportion of black families below the official poverty level fell from 56 per cent to 31 per cent between 1959 and 1972, overall black unemployment remained fairly constant at around 8 per cent; both poverty and unemployment continued to be twice as prevalent for blacks as for whites. Government, trade union and corporate training programmes are having some impact; black professional and technical employment increased 140 per cent during the 1960s, but still only accounted for 3·5 per cent in those fields. Particularly in the inner cities many blacks still constitute an unwanted and unskilled labour force.

Technological change is responsible for high regional unemployment. The Appalachian and Illinois coalfields have suffered from the decline of deep mining in favour of open-cast working employing large machines but few men (cf. Map 20). Partial exhaustion of the Superior iron-ore fields and reliance on new reserves, such as those in Labrador (cf. Map 26), has created severe problems in northern Minnesota and northern Michigan. The other large areas designated for redevelopment in 1961 reflected changes in some of the western mineral industries, difficulties in forestry and problems with some types of specialised farming. As with government contracts the general distribution of Redevelopment Area status was not entirely free from political pressures, which can further be seen in the inclusion of counties ranging from New York to Mississippi in the area under the Appalachian Commission.

Unfortunately the Economic Development Regions have not flourished. The Mexican-Americans and the Indians of the Four Corners in the southwest remain underprivileged and underemployed; the Ozarks and the Upper Great Lakes are isolated each in their own way, and all remain in need of better public facilities, more labour-training schemes and more jobs. Despite talk of a new era these regional commissions have been underfinanced and, being superimposed upon existing political structures, were given very little real power. However, their very existence makes the point that, despite the huge wealth of American society, vast areas and their peoples have been left behind in isolation and poverty, apparently neither wanted nor needed. Political power lies with the great urban-industrial centres, where concern focusses upon such issues as inflation, recession and energy rather than the plight of the distant poor.

51 Expenditure on education in the USA

The United States has a dual educational system: a hierarchy of private, fee-paying schools parallels the public system from kindergarten to college. In the public sector, which involves 87 per cent of all enrolment, control has traditionally been vested in state and local authorities with general supervision exercised by State Boards of Education; in most states the Board is appointed by the Governor, but in some it is elected. Each state is divided into school districts, over 16,000 throughout the country, administered by school boards either elected or appointed locally. Education is therefore very much under local control. However, greater federal concern with developing the national educational potential, together with a recent emphasis upon civil rights, has led to the provision of federal funds for the improvement of educational facilities, with consequent changes in intergovernmental relationships (cf. Map 52).

Expenditure on education forms by far the greatest item of expenditure by state and local governments, averaging 34 per cent of total spending compared with 18 per cent on public welfare, hospitals and health, and another 10 per cent on highways. Maps 51a and 51b plot expenditure on education *per capita* and per $1,000 of personal income. A comparison with Maps 50a and 50b shows a relationship between family income levels and educational spending, which, in *per capita* terms, is generally lowest in those states where median family incomes are depressed. Alabama and Arkansas are among the poorest states and spend relatively little *per capita* on education; wealthy states such as California, Michigan and New York have high *per capita* expenditures. In Rhode Island and Massachusetts educational expenditure in the public sector is not as high as might be expected in relation to median family income; this may reflect the strength of the private educational system in New England.

Per capita expenditure by itself does not adequately reflect the importance placed upon education. Education per $1,000 of personal income shows that even in the poorest states the level of spending is often comparable with that in wealthier states: California, for example, spends only a slightly larger proportion on education than Mississippi while some of the New England states spend significantly less; poor rural Arkansas spends more than the Manufacturing Belt states of Illinois, Indiana, Ohio or Pennsylvania. Whether or not the southern states regard the provision of high quality public schooling as an urgent social necessity, their low income characteristics are such that they may not be able to afford to improve their educational systems. Public schooling has always been seen as providing opportunity for upward economic and social mobility, but without specific federal funding for poor states, like impoverished inner cities, may be unable to help children escape from inherited poverty.

In rural America, particularly in the West, the level of expenditure is partly dictated by geographical conditions, for in some areas of scattered settlement educational costs are high. Cultural characteristics are also important. Minnesota's large North European immigrant population (cf. Map 11) has a

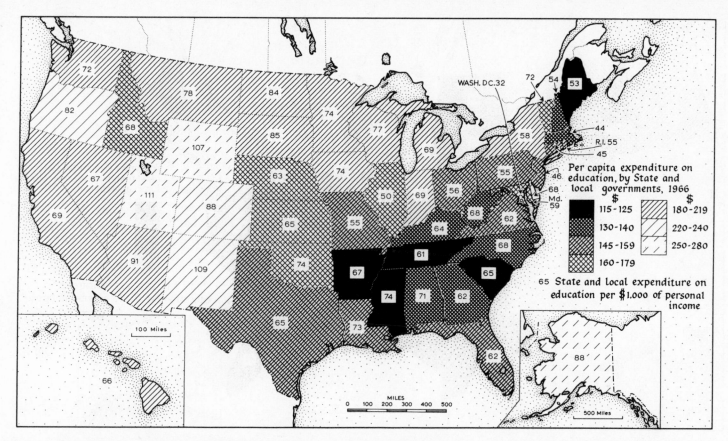

WASH. DC. 32

72   54   53
44
R.I. 55
45
46
68
Md.
59

72
78   84
82
74   77
68   85   69
107
63   74
67   111   88   50   69   56
69   65   55   64   68   62
91   109   74   67   61   68
65   74   71   62   65
73   62

58

55

Per capita expenditure on
education, by State and
local governments, 1966

$ $
115-125   180-219
130-140   220-240
145-159   250-280
160-179

65 State and local expenditure on
education per $1.000 of personal
income

100 Miles

66

MILES
0   100   200   300   400   500

88

500 Miles

51a » Expenditure on education in the public educational system of the USA, 1966

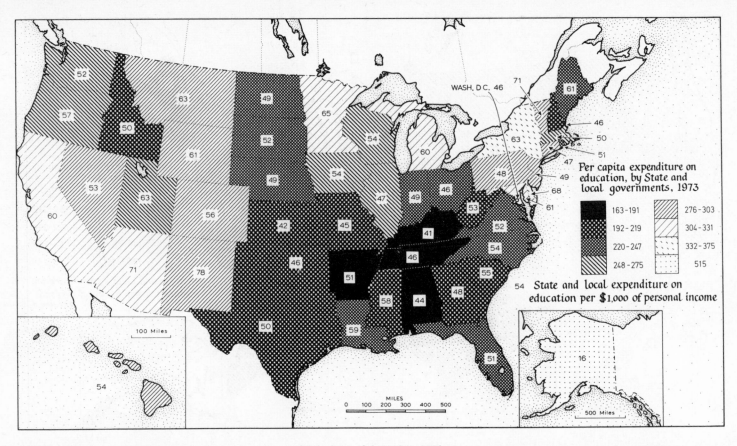

Per capita expenditure on
education, by State and
local governments, 1973

163-191
192-219
220-247
248-275
276-303
304-331
332-375
515

54 State and local expenditure on
education per $1,000 of personal income

WASH, D.C. 46

100 Miles

MILES
0 100 200 300 400 500

500 Miles

51b » Expenditure on education in the public educational system of the USA, 1973

tradition of providing public facilities such as education, which it is still able to support; in the Dakotas, by contrast, a decrease in general levels of prosperity has been reflected in a serious decline in proportionate support for education. Utah's support for public schooling may well reflect the enlightened traditions of the Mormon community in providing educational opportunity.

American colleges and universities likewise straddle the private and public sectors, although in this area a majority of 56 per cent are private. All the states provide higher educational facilities financed largely through the state legislatures, but the quality of these institutions varies widely: some have international reputations, but others have often been of only moderate academic quality. The statistics for educational expenditure in 1973 partly reflect this pattern of excellence, but also suggest that in such states as New York, where the state university system underwent massive expansion in the 1960s, the cost has been high. Given the fiscal problems of New York City, the economic limits upon such spending may well have been reached. The widely extreme figures for Alaska are due to unusually high cost-of-living in the present oil-boom conditions.

52 Segregation in the public schools of the American South

After the period of Reconstruction following the Civil War, southern whites were unable to accept the social, economic and political implications of the emancipation of the slaves. Continued desire to deny the equality of Afro-Americans produced a policy of segregation, in education as well as in other areas of public life. In the historic case of *Plessy* v *Ferguson* in 1896 the United States Supreme Court declared that segregation was constitutional, provided that Negro facilities were equal to those for whites. In 1954, in *Brown* v *the Board of Education*, the Court reversed the 'separate but equal' doctrine, declaring that the fact of separation was itself evidence of inequality; this decision provided the constitutional justification and stimulus for federal action to integrate the educational system.

Federal policy has been based upon Title VI of the Civil Rights Act of 1964: this prohibited racial discrimination in any programme or activity receiving federal funds, directed the federal agencies concerned to issue desegregation guidelines and authorised them to cut off funds from bodies that failed to comply. The Department of Health, Education and Welfare issued a series of such guidelines; and although senators from nine southern states asked for them to be revoked, President Johnson rejected their petition. The guidelines allowed school districts to comply with the 1964 act in one of three ways: by assurances of compliance, by court orders requiring desegregation or by submitting plans for desegregation. In January 1966

a survey by the Civil Rights Commission found that of the 4,941 school districts in the southern and border states, 2,755 had made assurances of compliance, 164 court orders had been filed and 1,904 desegregation plans received. A comparison between Maps 52a and 52b clearly shows the overall massive compliance throughout most of the South in recent years. Those states where relatively high levels of segregation remain are no longer those of the 'Deep South' but some of the border states, reflecting in part the *de facto* segregation of inner-city schoolchildren (cf. Map 40). Across the North the suburbanisation of the white urban population has left officially desegregated but often totally black schools in the inner-city segments of metropolitan areas. Thus in Illinois in 1973, 71 per cent of all black pupils attended schools that were at least 95 per cent black and in the particular case of the District of Columbia the proportion rose to 94 per cent. In moving to the suburbs, white Americans have often voted with their feet against multiracial schools. The only way to achieve integration in such circumstances is to transport children from one school district to another, but this policy runs counter to the established tradition of 'neighbourhood' schools. Though the practice of 'bussing' black children to keep schools segregated was long established in the rural South, the introduction of bussing to integrate schools, particularly in border and northern areas that thought the new rules applied only to the South, has often been met with widespread resistance. Black students trying to enter once all-white schools have been subjected to verbal abuse and physical violence, sufficient to require protection from law-enforcement agencies.

Such problems were also encountered in the southern states

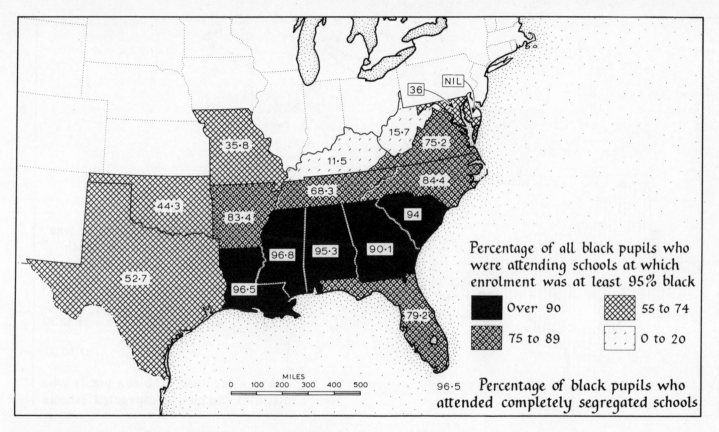

MILES
0   100 200 300 400 500

Percentage of all black pupils who were attending schools at which enrolment was at least 95% black

Over 90   55 to 74

75 to 89   0 to 20

96·5 Percentage of black pupils who attended completely segregated schools

52a » Segregation in the public schools of the American South, 1966

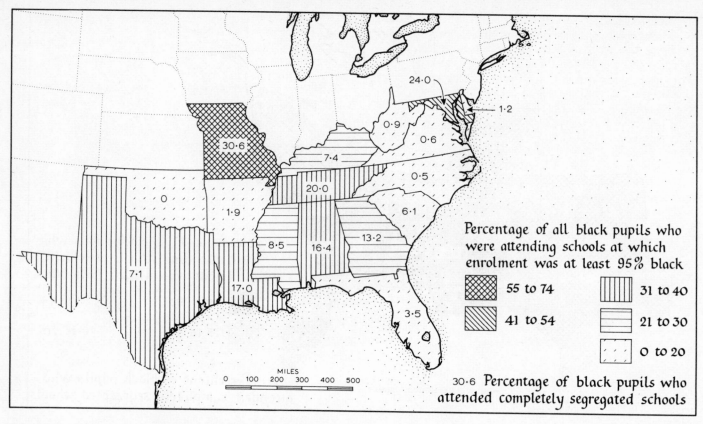

Percentage of all black pupils who were attending schools at which enrolment was at least 95% black

▨	55 to 74	▥	31 to 40
◪	41 to 54	▤	21 to 30
		░	0 to 20

30·6 Percentage of black pupils who attended completely segregated schools

MILES
0 100 200 300 400 500

52b » Segregation in the public schools of the American South, 1973

Map 52a illustrates the extent to which positive desegregation policy was necessary in the public primary and secondary schools of the seventeen southern and border states, excluding the District of Columbia, in 1966. The black population was generally more widely dispersed than in the North, and segregation was still the general rule. It declined in intensity from the 'Deep South' to the border states, partly because of different cultural conventions but also because of the increasing minority status of the black population (cf. Map 40). By December 1966 only 589,000 black pupils in the seventeen states attended schools that were less than 95 per cent black. By 1973 this had risen to over two million. During the same period the number of pupils attending completely segregated schools dropped from 2·5 million to just over 400,000. As Map 52b shows, the reversal was most dramatic in the five states that had been most segregated in 1966.

Opposition to bussing in many parts of the South, and the rapid expansion of private white schools, has received considerable attention, but after the initial clashes over desegregation policies there has been a remarkable degree of peaceful accommodation between blacks and whites. Remaining problems should not be allowed to overshadow the massive social change that has occurred throughout much of the South in a remarkably short time. The *de facto* segregation of the black population in many metropolitan areas, north and south, and hence of their education system, remains a much more intractable issue for American society.

53 Civil disorders in the American city

Violence has been a characteristic of American life since the early days of the frontier. The raw natural environment, conflict with the Indians, scattered settlement and the necessity for creating social, political and economic institutions in a relative 'wilderness' brought about a situation in which the gun emerged as a symbol of authority as well an an instrument of survival. With urbanisation the tensions and turbulence of an expanding, mobile and racially mixed society were intensified. The traditions of American life, with emphasis upon individual freedom, meant that the right of the citizen to bear arms became surrounded by claims of constitutional sanction. Although some states have gun-control legislation, congress did not act until after the assassinations of Martin Luther King, Jr and Robert F. Kennedy in 1968. Since 1900 over 800,000 US citizens have been killed by privately owned firearms, compared with 630,768 killed in war, but the act failed to require national registration of weapons. In the context of a society apparently tolerant of violence it is perhaps not surprising that the profound socio-economic frustrations of the black minority should find expression in violence, nor that white resentment of black advance should sometimes take the form of attack upon black persons and property.

Serious disorders involving blacks and whites occurred in both northern and southern cities in 1963 and 1964. A similar pattern emerged in 1965, with a major outburst in Watts, a black district in Los Angeles, where thirty-four persons were killed and $35 million of damage done; the National Guard were called out to restore order, and this became a typical response of law-enforcement authorities. Further disturbances in 1966 indicated that urban riots had become a regular feature of the American scene during the hot summer months. In 1967, eighty-three people died and 1,897 were injured: most of them were civilians.

Map 53 plots the distribution of civil disorders in 1967 according to the three categories established by the National Advisory Commission on Civil Disorders appointed by President Johnson. The Commission's mandate was to determine what happened, why it happened, and what could be done to prevent future outbreaks. According to the definition employed, there were between fifty-one and 217 disturbances in the first nine months of 1967. The Commission established 164, and ranked them by degree and duration. Eight disorders, or 5 per cent of the total, were major, characterised by numerous fires, intensive looting, reports of sniping, several days of violence, and the use of National Guard and/or federal forces as well as local police. Thirty-three disorders, 20 per cent, were classified as serious; the rest were minor, generally lasting for less than a day and quelled by local police.

Most disturbances occurred in the Manufacturing Belt, in cities with large black minorities, and the outbreaks cluster in and around metropolitan centres such as Newark, NJ and Detroit, Mich. Many of the riots were triggered by a specific incident, often trivial in itself, that tapped a reservoir of grievance and tension. The Detroit riot, in which there were forty-three deaths and between $40 and $50 million of damage,

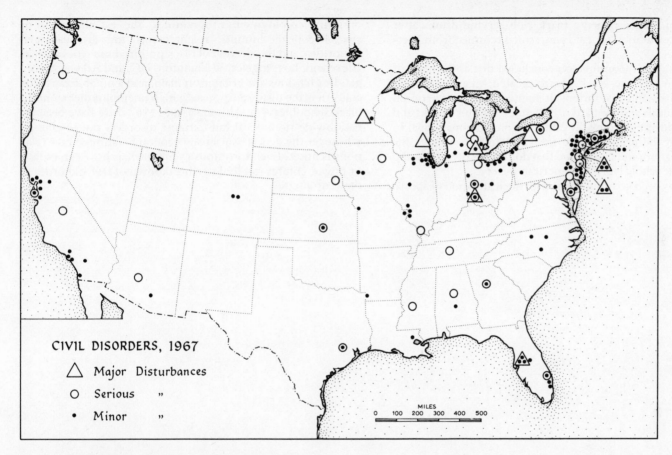

CIVIL DISORDERS, 1967

△ Major Disturbances

○ Serious   "

• Minor   "

MILES

0   100 200 300 400 500

53 » Civil disorders in the American city, 1967

began when police raided a black club serving drinks after hours at a celebration for two servicemen returned from Vietnam.

The President's Commission concluded that at the heart of the problem lay the black ghetto created, maintained, and condoned by white institutions. It pointed to the gulf between American ideals and the hard reality of life for most blacks and other low-income groups. It called for programmes equal to the scale of the problems, for new initiatives to change the system of failure and frustration that dominates the ghetto and weakens the whole fabric of American society.

Much has been accomplished, with the instigation of special minority employment programmes, the establishment of special college entrance requirements for disadvantaged minorities, and the election of black politicians in cities such as Cleveland, Los Angeles, Washington, DC, and Atlanta, Georgia. But tensions and frictions remain, and a notable cause for concern is the disproportionately high unemployment among black school leavers. Although since 1967 there have been no nationwide riots, local but extreme disorders can re-emerge whenever the delicate social and economic fabric of race relations is upset. Even fortuitous events such as heavy snowfalls or power failures can lead to a breakdown of law and order in the central cities.

54 Political representation in the USA

In the early years of the Republic political parties were regarded as factions and disruptive; however, they soon came to be seen as essential instruments for the smooth manipulation of the political process. In the nineteenth century two major parties emerged which, despite numerous third-party movements, have managed to retain a controlling influence. Essentially non-ideological and pragmatic, the Republicans and Democrats have frequently been distinguished by different concepts of the federal-state relationship: Republicans have traditionally emphasised individualism and localism, whilst the Democratic party has been more prepared to accept extensions of federal authority in the interest both of the 'general welfare' and its own political fortunes.

The Constitution provides that in the upper house of federal legislature, the senate, each state shall have equal representation without regard to differences in area or population. Senators are elected for terms lasting six years, with a third of the senate membership elected every two years. In the house of representatives the 435 members are apportioned among the states in relation to population. Each state has a minimum of one congressman (e.g. Nevada), and the largest delegations come from the most populous states, California and New York. Each congressman serves two years, and the entire membership of the house of representatives comes up for re-election every two years. The frequency of congressional elections provides a useful barometer for measuring changes in political attitudes among the electorate.

Since 1945 there has consistently been a higher percentage of voters identifying themselves as Democrats rather than Republicans, with large numbers, ranging from a fifth to a third of the electorate, professing independence of party. These independents clearly influence election results and partly explain the split patterns between presidential and congressional elections, patterns that are further complicated if elections to state governorships and other offices are also taken into account. The general balance of party strength, in terms of the measures shown on Map 54, is fairly typical of recent years. With the exception of the periods 1947 to 1949 and 1953 to 1955, the Democratic Party has controlled both houses of congress. Regional and income-group voting behaviour have, however, become increasingly more complex in recent years as a result of minority-rights issues and the greater uncertainties about economic and foreign affairs. No longer does the Democratic Party rule the 'solid South' as a one party section, nor dominate the northern industrial cities and states as it did for thirty years following the Great Depression.

The narrow Republican victory in the 1968 presidential election can be explained largely by Democratic divisions over the Vietnam war, and the landslide re-election of Richard Nixon in 1972 by the apparent success of his foreign policies and by popular rejection of the outspoken liberal Democratic nominee, George McGovern. Carter's nomination in 1976 was a triumph of persistent effort and disarray among his Democratic rivals. In the election itself he won by only narrow margins that underlined the diminished power of the old

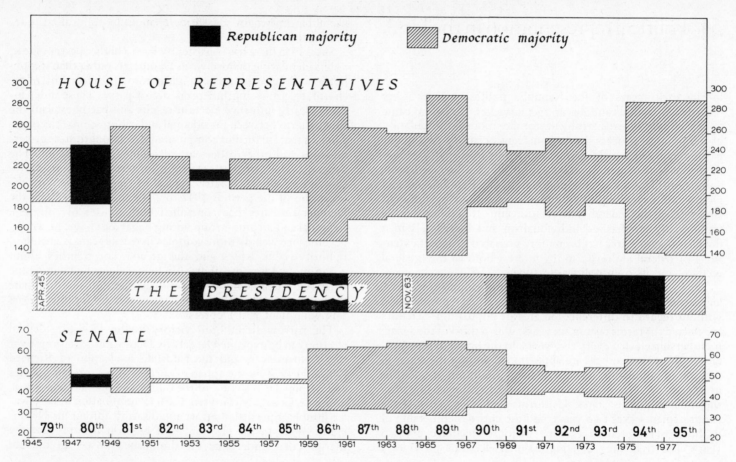

HOUSE OF REPRESENTATIVES

THE PRESIDENCY

APR 45

NOV 63

SENATE

| 79th | 80th | 81st | 82nd | 83rd | 84th | 85th | 86th | 87th | 88th | 89th | 90th | 91st | 92nd | 93rd | 94th | 95th |

1945　1947　1949　1951　1953　1955　1957　1959　1961　1963　1965　1967　1969　1971　1973　1975　1977

54a ≫ Political representation in the USA, 95th Congress

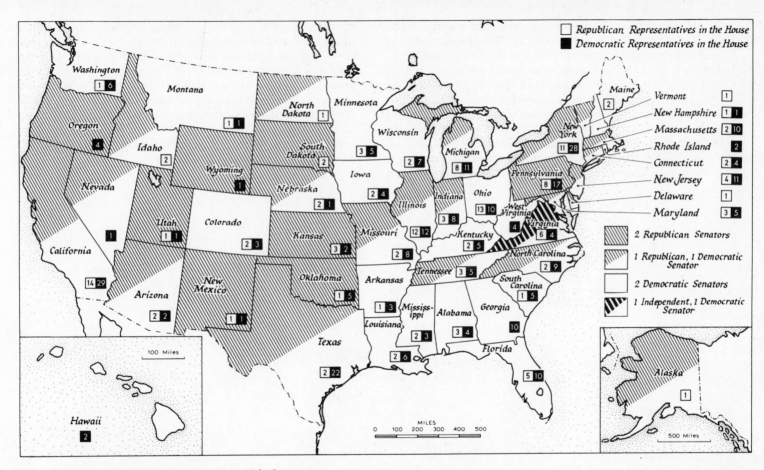

54b » Political representation in the USA, 95th Congress

Democratic coalition to deliver the votes, even at a time when the Watergate scandal continued, at least theoretically, to weaken Republican support. A feature of the 95th Congress was that more than half its members had first been elected within the past decade, and a third had held office for three years or less. These new and younger members achieved significant reforms in congressional organisation, particularly with regard to the seniority system that had given conservative Southern Democrats control of both houses. This has been eroded, although not destroyed. Increased problems of party discipline and the post-Watergate, post-Vietnam desire to re-establish legislative control over the executive, coupled with the Carter administration's inexperience in dealing with Capital Hill, have magnified political problems in Washington. This has been well illustrated by Congress's rejection of Carter's energy proposals and by its own failure to develop a coherent and acceptable alternative. Complex issues of foreign policy such as the SALT II treaty also underline the difficulty of policy formulation in a federal state covering an enormous geographical area with strong democratic traditions and a developed socio-economic structure.

55 Political representation in Canada

The governmental system of the Dominion of Canada embodies elements of both British and American practice. Like the United States, Canada is a federal union that has grown through the accession of new areas (cf. Map 5), and now embraces eleven provinces and the northern territories. It has developed, however, within the framework of the British empire and commonwealth, and its parliamentary procedures are modelled on those of Westminster. The governor-general, appointed on the recommendation of the Canadian prime minister, is the representative of the British Crown, the unifying symbol of the three branches of the federal government, and the legal point of reference on questions of disputed authority.

The Parliament of Canada is bicameral, consisting of an elected house of commons and an appointed senate. Provincial representation in the house is proportional to population, and re-apportionment follows the decennial census; current membership is 264, which has risen to 282 after the May 1979 election; this redistribution, the first since 1966, is based on the 1971 census. Senators, who used to be appointed on the advice of the prime minister for life have, since 1965, been required to retire at the age of seventy-five. They now number 104: Ontario and Quebec each have twenty-four senators; there are six from each of the four western provinces, ten each from Nova Scotia and New Brunswick, four from Prince Edward Island, six from Newfoundland and one each from the Northwest Territories and the Yukon. The federal judiciary comprises a Supreme Court and a Federal Court which, since 1970, has replaced the Exchequer Court of Canada. Criminal law is under the legislative authority of Parliament but civil law remains under provincial control and English traditions prevail except in Quebec, which retains a version of the French code introduced when the province formed part of the French empire in North America. The prime minister and his cabinet, the executive branch of the Dominion government, represent prevailing majorities in the house of commons.

At Canada's request, the British North America Act of 1867 was revised in 1949 to give the Dominion government greater authority, except in relation to provincial and educational rights and rights to the use of the French and English languages. Between 1968 and 1971 eight federal-provincial conferences were held to explore a new constitution but the subsequent Canadian Constitutional Charter of 1971 failed to win acceptance at a constitutional conference held in Vancouver. Agreement has not yet been reached on the final transfer of jurisdiction from Westminster to Ottawa, which requires the unanimous consent of all provinces. Quebec's insistence on special status within the Confederation has created difficulties that are yet to be resolved. However, the adoption of a new flag in 1965, replacing the modified version of the Red Ensign, symbolised the growing sense of Canadian national identity. The strength of opinion in Quebec was recognised in 1969 when Parliament passed the Official Languages Act which declared that French and English enjoyed equal status and were equally to be the official languages of Canada. Bilingualism has

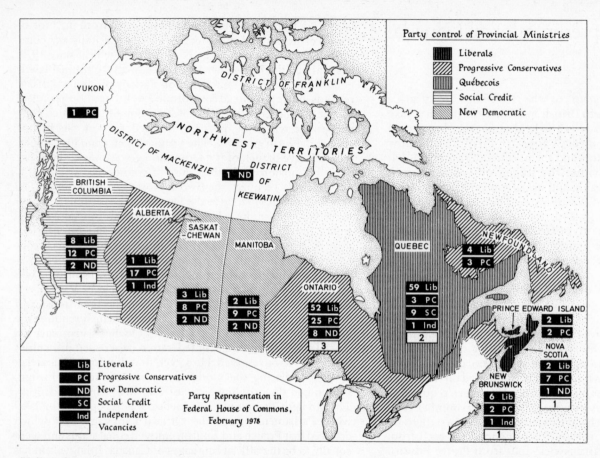

Party control of Provincial Ministries

- Liberals
- Progressive Conservatives
- Québecois
- Social Credit
- New Democratic

YUKON
1 PC

DISTRICT OF FRANKLIN

NORTHWEST TERRITORIES

DISTRICT OF MACKENZIE

DISTRICT OF KEEWATIN

1 ND

BRITISH COLUMBIA
8 Lib
12 PC
2 ND
1

ALBERTA
1 Lib
17 PC
1 Ind

SASKAT-CHEWAN
3 Lib
8 PC
2 ND

MANITOBA
2 Lib
9 PC
2 ND

ONTARIO
52 Lib
25 PC
8 ND
3

QUEBEC
59 Lib
3 PC
9 SC
1 Ind
2

NEWFOUNDLAND
4 Lib
3 PC

PRINCE EDWARD ISLAND
2 Lib
2 PC

NOVA SCOTIA
2 Lib
7 PC
1 ND
1

NEW BRUNSWICK
6 Lib
2 PC
1 Ind
1

Lib Liberals
PC Progressive Conservatives
ND New Democratic
SC Social Credit
Ind Independent
Vacancies

Party Representation in
Federal House of Commons,
February 1978

not, however, satisfied the movement within Quebec for separatism.

In the provincial elections of November 1976 Quebec cast 41 per cent of its votes to the Parti Québecois, enough to defeat the ruling Liberal Party and give power to what had formerly been a splinter group dedicated to Quebec independence. The election of René Lévesque as premier of Quebec has led to a power struggle with the Liberal federal prime minister, Pierre Trudeau, whose Liberal Party continued to dominate the federal house of commons, until defeated in 1979. Quebec, with 80 per cent of its population of 4·8 million French speaking, is in conflict with majority opinion in a Dominion of twenty-three million people of whom nearly 75 per cent have English as their first or only language. But the province is rich in economic resources and contributes 23 per cent of Canada's total GNP. By this index alone it would, if independent, rank twenty-third among the world's wealthiest nations.

Ex-Prime Minister Trudeau, elected in 1968 with an image comparable to that of John F. Kennedy in the United States, found his position consistently threatened by Québecois separatism, and the policy of official bilingualism has upset the predominantly English-speaking western provinces. The struggle for power has resulted in a softening of Quebec's separatist platform in favour of 'sovereignty-association' and monetary and economic union with the rest of Canada. The new governor-general of Canada, Edward Schreyer, has vigorously defended the federal principle and believes that the distinctive Francophone culture of Quebec can fully be expressed within the wider Dominion. Meanwhile Premier Lévesque continues to view the Confederation as an 'obsolete contraption' and remains opposed to proposals for constitutional reform.

56 The strategy of Cold War, 1945-75

After 1945 international politics came to be dominated by ideological conflict between capitalism and communism, focussed on rivalry between the United States and the Soviet Union. Modern technology, making possible almost instant communication and presenting the threat of instant destruction, conditioned the foreign policies of these two 'superpowers' away from direct confrontation towards more covert manoeuvring for strategic position. Each sought to extend its influence, and that of its political and economic system, within the context of established interstate relationships, and the major threats to international peace occurred at zones of conflict around the perimeters of the rival alliance systems. Map 56 shows the post-war pattern of American diplomacy and, using an azimuthal projection centred on Delhi, illustrates the encompassing nature of the American alliance structure. Eurasia is shown as the 'world heartland', and the communist core is almost surrounded by countries allied with the United States.

The key to American policy was the theory of 'containment' enunciated in 1947. Believing that communism was an expanding system aimed at world domination the United States sought to achieve military superiority over the Soviet Union, whilst at the same time preventing communist encroachment into the 'west' by a programme of economic and military assistance to nations whose stability seemed in doubt. A global alliance structure became an essential ingredient of containment. The Inter-American Treaty signed at Rio de Janeiro in 1947 by the United States and twenty Latin American Republics established the Organisation of American States and reaffirmed the principle that the western hemisphere should be inviolate from external intervention. In 1949 the North Atlantic Treaty was signed by the United States, Canada and ten European nations, later to be joined by three others. NATO was a military alliance for mutual security, providing a collective shield for Europe, behind which the allies rebuilt the European economy. The hope that this dual policy would re-invigorate the European politico-economic structure was justified. NATO survived the withdrawal of French forces in 1967, and economic co-operation bore fruit in the European Economic Community.

The Soviet response to NATO was the Warsaw Pact, concluded in 1955 between the USSR, Albania, Bulgaria, Czechoslovakia, East Germany, Hungary, Poland and Rumania. With almost two million communist forces balanced against slightly over one million NATO forces, Europe enjoyed uneasy peace. Spain was not a member of NATO, but in 1955 concluded a defence agreement with the United States that permitted American bases in Spain in exchange for economic and military aid. Some members of NATO were also members of the Central Treaty Organisation (CENTO) of 1959, which formed a link between NATO and the South East Asia Treaty Organisation (SEATO).

SEATO was established in 1954 to provide for collective defence and economic co-operation. It reflected increasing concern with the policies of Communist China, and the provi-

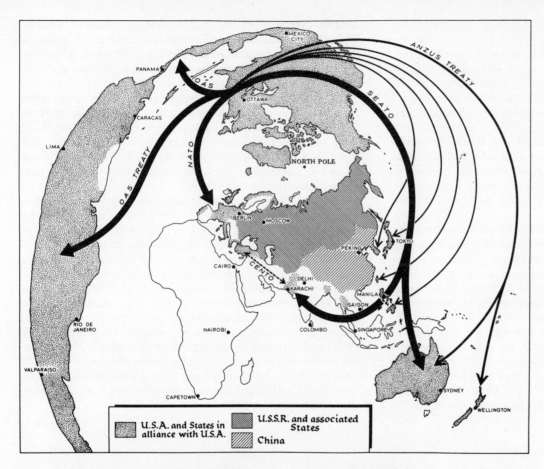

The following labels appear on the map:

MEXICO CITY
PANAMA
OAS
CARACAS
OTTAWA
NORTH POLE
LIMA
OAS TREATY
NATO
BERLIN
MOSCOW
SEATO
ANZUS TREATY
CAIRO
CENTO
DELHI
KARACHI
PEKING
TOKYO
MANILA
SAIGON
RIO DE JANEIRO
NAIROBI
COLOMBO
SINGAPORE
VALPARAISO
CAPETOWN
SYDNEY
WELLINGTON

Legend:

U.S.A. and States in alliance with U.S.A.

U.S.S.R. and associated States

China

56 » The strategy of Cold War, 1945–75

sions of the treaty formed part of the American justification for intervention in South Vietnam. The American defence perimeter in the Far East was also defined by bilateral security agreements with Japan (1951), South Korea (1953), the Republic of China (1954) and the Philippines (1951). Links with Australia and New Zealand were formalised in the ANZUS Treaty of 1951. A large part of the world was therefore embraced by the two rival power blocs.

In the great belt of non-aligned 'Third World' countries Africa came to look increasingly exposed as the old European empires were dismantled. By the mid-1960s it had become an arena for great power politics and covert intervention, although initially modest, had become intensified by the mid-1970s.

Events in the 1960s and early 1970s, however, were dominated by restlessness in the Soviet Union's Eastern European satellites, by continuing tensions leading to periodic wars between Arabs and Israelis in the Middle East and by American intervention in South East Asia. The Vietnam War was, in many ways, the ultimate military expression of containment theory as it had been practised for twenty years. Inability to force a military solution in South Vietnam led eventually to total withdrawal. In this context, since the early 1970s, successive American administrations have pursued policies of *détente* towards the Soviet Union that have been paralleled by a *rapprochement* with the People's Republic of China. Normalisation of relations with the PRC has involved abrogation of the bilateral arrangement with the Republic of China on Taiwan. These developments, together with the earlier dismantling of SEATO, represent a revolution in US Far Eastern policy and total rejection of the stategic and diplomatic patterns of the era of Cold War.

Elsewhere the CENTO alliance is unlikely to survive in any form following government changes in both Pakistan and Iran. NATO remains intact as the dominant expression of the North Atlantic partnership, but in the western hemisphere the rapidity of economic development in Latin America, and acceptance of the legitimacy of the Cuban revolution of 1959, have changed the nature of the OAS.

Map 56 illustrates a world view that embodied a global strategy that has been eroded under pressure of events. It has been replaced by recognition of the pluralistic and diverse nature of the world community, and the fluidity of an international environment in which cultural nationalism is again an assertive force and economic interdependence a reality. Vietnam demonstrated the fragility of imposed military solutions. The energy crisis underlines the limitations on the concept of superpower which is self-defined in industrial and military terms. Soviet-American tensions remain and find expression in many geographical areas and over many issues. The replacement of confrontation policies by *détente* does not solve world problems, but rejection of the classic simplifications of the period of Cold War may offer greater scope for constructive statesmanship.